THE CLASSIC CAR

— SPOTTERS' GUIDE —

WHAT TO SEE AT BRITAIN'S CAR SHOWS

NICK EVANS

First published 2023

The History Press
97 St George's Place, Cheltenham,
Gloucestershire, GL50 3QB
www.thehistorypress.co.uk

British Library Cataloguing in Publication Data.
A catalogue record for this book is available from the British
Library.

ISBN 978 0 7509 9423 1

Typesetting and origination by The History Press
Printed in Turkey by IMAK

Cover illustrations
Front, from top left: MGA, MGB and MG
T-Type sports cars come to the fore
in east Kent; Jaguar E-Types make a
dominating presence near Sandwich,
Kent; Classic original Minis on parade near
Faversham, Kent.
Back: A 1970 Vauxhall Viva HB and a
1970 MGC GT share some of the limelight
at the Festival Of The Unexceptional
in Lincolnshire.

AUTHOR'S INTRODUCTION

The Classic Car Spotter's Guide is a chance to take off our hats to all the men and women who spend endless hours maintaining, fettling, polishing and showing off their cherished classic cars so that we get the chance to enjoy them as much as they do.

You will see them, both cars and owners – or custodians, depending on your point of view – at any of the myriad classic car shows up and down the country during spring and summer weekends.

In the best of British weather, hundreds of older motors will be lined up for us to admire in serried ranks on parks, playing fields, village greens or closed-off town centres. Some cars are positively slavered over while others cut no ice with passers-by – perhaps they are just a tad too familiar still – but have we considered how much we really know about these transports of delight?

The definition of a classic car is open ended and many a lively pub discussion has been had about the deciding factors. I've taken the line that a model of car should have been launched on to the British market since 1945 and before 1985 to appear in this book. Sometimes, for illustration, it's been necessary to feature an example that is more recent but whose production began before 1985.

It would be easy to dismiss the classic car scene as a minority hobby but to do so would be a serious mistake. The most recent five-yearly survey, produced by the Federation of Historic British Vehicles, suggests there are now more than 1.5 million classic cars on our roads, owned by 700,000 people, and the value they contribute to the British economy is over £10 billion. A second and more detailed report, by the Centre for Economics and Business Research, put that figure at £18 billion. I sometimes feel I have given a large chunk of that single-handedly when my MGB has needed fettling!

The federation also noted that 4,000 businesses in Britain, supporting more than 34,000 jobs, are involved in the classic car industry one way or another – that's people who are buying, selling, maintaining, repairing or restoring older cars as well as making or supplying spare parts and, yes, even writing about them.

Here then is your jovial, yet not technical, companion to learning more about some of the most popular models you can find at a car show – some 41 per cent of the UK's classics are former British Leyland/British Motor Corporation marques. However, all of them will hold special memories, whether it was a first car, family runabout, rep's special, a passion wagon or because a mate of yours, heaven forfend, put one in a ditch on the way home after a raucous session in the Dog & Duck!

Look out too for the rarity ratings by each car's profile – with stars awarded for the likelihood (or not) of actually seeing one in the metal at a show near you. A single star denotes the most common models, while five stars means you are looking at something very rare.★

Happy spotting, and if you have bought this book, thank you for contributing to my MG's spare parts fund!

Nick Evans
Whitstable, April 2023

★ Stars are awarded on the author's entirely fallible opinion and are completely unscientific!

ACKNOWLEDGEMENTS

Publications consulted during the writing of this book include the series of *Cars We Loved* books by Giles Chapman, *Great British Cars* by Stephen Barnett and various issues of the *Classic Car Buyer* newspaper. Data about remaining vehicle numbers was sourced from the website How Many Left?, www.howmanyleft.co.uk.

The author would like to thank the owners of the cars featured throughout the book for allowing them to be photographed. Unless otherwise stated, all photos were taken by the author.

With thanks also to the organisers of the Festival of the Unexceptional, the British Motor Show, the London Classic Car Show, Classic Music & Motors events in east Kent and Hobbs Parker Auctions of Ashford, Kent.

CITROËN 2CV

1948–88

As much a part of the French way of life as a beret and a baguette, the Citroën 2CV brought cheap motoring to the masses for, on and off, half a century.

The very first ones, a batch of 250, were built just before the start of the Second World War and were quickly hidden away when the German army came calling in 1940.

Famously designed to be driven by peasants across a ploughed field, one of whom had to carry a tray of eggs on their lap without

You can expect to see a line-up of tin snails at most local classic car shows. Around 3,000 remain in Britain, according to How Many Left?

breaking them, it wouldn't be until the Paris Motor Show of 1948 that this little car saw the light of day again.

The Deux Chevaux – for that is what 2CV means – or two horses, is as basic as a car can be. All of them were fitted with a canvas roll-back sunroof, lively suspension and deckchair seats – pulled along through the front wheels by a two-cylinder, 602cc, air-cooled engine.

The first ones sold in Britain were actually built here during the 1950s at Citroën's Slough factory, alongside the Light 15, to avoid import tariffs. Ultimately, this proved too costly and production ceased by the end of the decade.

It wouldn't be until 1974 that we would see the tin snail sold new on our shores again, prompted by a thirst for economy motors after the previous year's oil crisis. Imported from France and sold for £830 each, they quickly found new homes – most notably among *Guardian* readers, vegetarians and people who liked wearing cheesecloth.

Production ceased in 1988 and a number of limited editions, in two-tone colours, were built as the finale approached. The survival rate of these later cars is good and you should spot one or two easily enough at local shows. Earlier ones succumbed to the dreaded tin worm, while UK-built examples are all but extinct.

An early example of a Citroën 2CV – note the absence of rear quarterlight windows.

A later example of the 2CV van. Only twenty or so vans are thought to be on our roads now.

RARITY RATING

★★★ 1980S EXAMPLES
★★★★ ALL OTHERS

CITROËN LIGHT 15/ TRACTION AVANT

1948–57

Mars bars are probably the most famous thing to come out of the Berkshire town of Slough, but second place can go to Citroëns built at the company's plant in the town during the late 1940s and '50s.

The Light 15, as it was officially known in the UK, was the right-hand-drive version of the Traction Avant, a mainstay for French Citroën since 1934.

The Avant, widely used today in TV dramas depicting wartime and 1950s Paris, was the world's first front-wheel-drive monocoque production car. It had originally been designed by André Lefèbvre and Flaminio Bertoni in late 1933. Production of the Light 15 was slated to begin at Slough later in the 1930s, but it was immediately put on hold at the outbreak of war in 1939.

A near-pristine example of a Slough-built Citroën Light 15, resplendent in Rolls-Royce red – a colour offered by Citroën in the early 1950s.

A walnut veneer fascia helped differentiate British Tractions from their less well-appointed French-built cousins.

Headlight and wing mirror details. Lucas electrical items were fitted to Slough-made Light 15s.

The British cars had to consist of 51 per cent UK components to avoid import duties, which was a major issue in the post-war era with the government keen to protect the home car industry. By the time Light 15 production came to an end in 1957, some 26,400 had been built in Slough (out of a total of 760,000 made worldwide). The Slough-built cars used 12V Lucas electrics, headlights, dynamo and starter motor with Jaeger instruments and a walnut dashboard.

There has long been some debate over whether French or British models were better. The British 15s featured leather seats and walnut fascia, as well as more robust electrical systems, pointing to greater luxury and reliability.

Today, the Light 15s/Tractions still retain a great deal of kerb appeal, particularly among those keen to recreate vintage settings of French detectives and bejewelled ladies of the night!

RARITY RATING

★★★★ ALL MODELS

LAND ROVER

1948–2016

In 1947, after one of the most severe winters of the century to date, a chap called Maurice Wilks bought himself a war-surplus US Army Jeep to tow away fallen trees from his farm driveway.

The weather didn't improve, so the Jeep came in handy to get to the local shops. Eventually, when the grey clouds cleared, the vehicle came into its own again for Maurice to take his family for a weekend break at Red Dwarf Bay in Anglesey. There, Maurice was joined by his brother Spencer, who was general manager of Rover, a company struggling to meet the needs of the export-hungry post-war car market.

In a lightbulb moment, they realised there was nothing to replace the Jeep – unless Rover stepped in to build its own version of this go-anywhere, do-anything vehicle. Maurice and Spencer even drew their first sketches on the sands of the beach that weekend.

Thus was born the Land Rover. The development programme, Project J, was rushed through so that a finished model could make its debut at the Amsterdam Motor Show in 1948. The farming market – desperate to invest in new machinery and equipment – seized the opportunity. Rover had budgeted for building 100 Land Rovers a week but before the end of that year production had ramped up to 500 a week. That had doubled again by 1950, with exports to seventy countries around the world.

Rover's future was assured as it carved out big slices of this new off-road market. Even wartime Prime Minister Sir Winston Churchill bought one for his estate at Chartwell, near Westerham in Kent.

This short-wheelbase Land Rover has four sideways-facing rear seats. Passengers would not necessarily have travelled in comfort!

Land Rover's boiler plate declared the vehicle was a four-wheel-drive station wagon, above all else.

By the late 1950s, the Series II Land Rover had arrived – effectively the vehicle the Wilks brothers had dreamed of back on the beach ten years earlier – which smoothed out a lot of the earlier Landy's quirks, offered a better ride and made for a more aesthetically pleasing design, penned now by David Bache.

Land Rovers were available in different wheelbases and body styles, making them easy to convert for any purpose, not always by Rover but by a growing number of specialists. An early adopter was the Automobile Association, which bought Series Is for its patrols in the Scottish Highlands and central London. Others were converted into police vehicles, military patrol carriers, fire engines and TV relay trucks, as well as being the tool of choice for the competitors in Camel Trophy expeditions.

The AA bought a number of Series I Land Rovers during the early 1950s for its patrols in central London and the Scottish Highlands. This one made it into preservation.

On perhaps a darker note, the Land Rover also became a symbol of authority as used by police and armed forces around the world to quell riots and to round up troublemakers (or beat them up in the cases of South Africa and Rhodesia (now Zimbabwe)).

In the early 1990s, British Telecom, which had a fleet of safety-yellow-painted Landies, decided to change its corporate colour to grey. In Northern Ireland, still getting over the worst of the Troubles, staff feared that resprayed grey ones could be confused for army vehicles and make them a soft target. Happily, it seems those fears were largely unfounded.

The spartan interior of the preserved AA patrol Land Rover. Note the radio hand piece and loudspeaker.

By 1990, which saw the launch of the Defender models, Land Rover was primed to capitalise on a growing off-road leisure market, despite varying build quality that had harmed export sales. BMW acquired the off-road marque when it took over Rover, later selling it on to Ford who, by 2008, moved it on to Tata Group to integrate it with Jaguar. Their successive significant investments have ensured Land Rover vehicles are widely respected today, although there was considerable consternation when the largely hand-built Defender ceased production in 2016 to make way for the new models that have appeared since.

Early Land Rovers are rare, with Series I and II models commanding strong prices. Look out for versions displayed at local shows by off-road groups, some no doubt exhibiting their military past. More modern ones are set to become classics of the future.

RARITY RATING

★★★ DEFENDER AND COUNTY MODELS
★★★★ SERIES I AND II MODELS
★★★★ SPECIALIST CONVERSIONS

MORRIS MINOR

1948–70

Beloved by district nurses and many others throughout the land for its simplicity and ruggedness, the Morris Minor and its variants were a firm fixture of Britain's golden age of motoring in the 1950s and '60s – thousands still chug around now, their distinctive engine tone marking them out from a distance.

Commercial versions of the Minor sometimes wore the Austin badge instead of Morris. Pick-ups – complete with rear canvas-framed top – are rare on our roads today. This well-looked-after example was in search of a new home when spotted at a classic car auction.

The neat engine layout of a later 1960s Morris Minor. All the major under-bonnet components are readily to hand for routine maintenance.

One of Britain's most revered popular classic cars is the Morris Minor Traveller – aka the half-timbered car.

The Minor's launch at the Earls Court Motor Show in October 1948 was nothing short of a post-war recovery sensation and it was the first car to be designed by Alec Issigonis. His concept was that the car should be affordable, practical and economical. 'The average man,' he said at the time, 'would take pleasure in owning it, rather than feeling it was something he had been sentenced to.'

Development started during the war years under the code name Mosquito. Issigonis wanted the car to be spacious and comfortable for inexperienced motorists, so prime concerns were excellent roadholding and accurate steering. Unitary construction – a first for Morris – and independent suspension were among the innovations that made it to manufacture.

With production dates already set, Issigonis ordered the car to be made 4in wider to improve its looks. The bodyshell and running gear were hastily adapted. Telltale signs of these changes were the bonnet, whose machine pressing was altered by inserting a 4in-wide strip down the middle, and the first batch of bumpers, which had a plate welded into their centres.

An estate, or Traveller, version became available in 1952 and, thanks to its half-timbered shooting-brake styling, became as legendary as the saloon. Today, the Traveller is arguably more popular with classic owners. New parts are readily found and all variants can be rebuilt from the ground up by specialist companies to customers' requirements.

At launch, the Minor was fitted with a 918cc engine, which was replaced by a more efficient Austin-based 803cc version after Morris's merger with that company in 1952. An improved A-series 948cc engine became standard equipment from 1956 onwards, giving rise to the Morris 1000 name. Flat out, the car could reach 75mph and achieve 0–60mph in a steady 31.3 seconds.

The Minor has the distinction of being the first British car to sell a million, which it achieved by December 1960. This milestone was marked by producing 360 lilac-painted models the following year, badged as Minor Millions. It's an odd number to build but easily explained by there being one supplied to every Morris dealer at the time.

The van version – some of which actually carried Austin badges – became the mainstay of many corporate fleets, most notably with the Post Office, who had red ones for Royal Mail and green ones for its telephones division (Post Office Telephones later became British Telecom). Some examples of the latter survive with a complete engineers' kit and prove a popular draw at car shows.

By the time production came to an end in 1971 for the saloons and 1972 for the van and Traveller, 1,368,291 examples had been built across global markets. Some 23,000 are thought to still be on and off British roads now, according to How Many Left?

RARITY RATING

★★   SALOONS AND TRAVELLERS
★★★   VANS AND CONVERTIBLES
★★★★ PICK-UPS

Right: A line of Minors (and a Morris Oxford furthest away from the camera).

AUSTIN A30 & A35

1951–68

Unveiled at the Earls Court Motor Show in October 1951 as a reply to the Morris Minor, the A30, or New Seven, was the smallest of Austin's range of curvy cars that became typical of the decade.

Adverts at the time showed four adults riding in comfort, but the reality proved a bit of a squeeze if you were more than average height.

That didn't stop people flocking to see this new motor, viewed by Austin as a modern person's car. Priced at £504 including tax, it was £24 cheaper than the Minor, largely because a heater, second windscreen wiper and passenger-side sun visor were optional extras. The A30 was Austin's first car with unitary construction and the electrics were 12V, at a time when 6V was the norm for the majority of cars.

The Austin A30 was the company's first car to be built with unitary construction.

Most notable, though, was its 803cc, 30bhp, four-cylinder engine, which would make its own mark on the British motor industry. Beefed up to 948cc to return a creditable 42mpg in 1956, three years after the Austin–Morris merger, the power plant would become the A-series engine. It would be the heart of countless BMC and British Leyland vehicles, such as the Mini, Minor, Healey Sprite and 1100. Further developed versions would later be fitted into the Allegro, Metro, Maestro and Montego, staying in production until 2000.

In 1956, the A30 was given a facelift to become the A35, fitted with that improved 948cc engine too. This version can be readily identified by its larger rear window and painted grille – which had previously been chrome.

Van and Countryman estate versions, both featuring squared-off back end and hinged side-opening rear door, would also be common sights on Britain's roads for years after. The saloon gave way to the Farina-designed A40 in 1959 but the van kept going until 1968, later finding retro fame as Wallace & Gromit's mode of transport in their stop-motion animated films.

When production ended at Longbridge, some 450,000 A30s and A35s had been made. Around 3,900 remain on and off our roads now, according to the statistics on How Many Left?

The 948cc engine of a 1959 Austin A35 – simplicity itself.

Speedo, fuel gauge and warning lights are accommodated in one central position on a body-coloured metal dashboard. Map light and radio are no doubt later additions.

RARITY RATING

★★★ SALOONS
★★★★ VAN AND ESTATE MODELS

VOLKSWAGEN BEETLE

1952–80 (IN THE UK)

It must rank as the British motor industry's greatest blunder of the age. What if Sir William Rootes, co-director with brother Sir Reginald of the successful Rootes Group – manufacturer of Hillman, Humber and Singer cars – had decided after all that he did like the look of a quirky German car offered to him on a plate and believed it would sell by the million?

Picture this: the Second World War has just ended and the Allies are picking through what's left of a razed Germany to get the country and swathes of mainland Europe back on their feet again. The British Army has acquired a large factory in Lower Saxony that has been building military vehicles and has discovered the pressings and tooling for a small family car.

Seen in full Herbie the Love Bug livery is this well-cared-for Beetle, which was one of seven built for the 1969 Disney film. This example was fitted with a Porsche engine and improved suspension for use in high-speed scenes.

There were enough subtle design changes made to the Beetle by the late 1960s for it to look quite different from those of twenty years earlier. By the 1970s, windscreens would be curved rather than flat.

Major Ivan Hirst of the Army of Occupation is running the plant, which by March 1946 had made its 1,000th car and is offering the operation to a mainstream manufacturer.

We shall never know the answer to that 'what if' question because Sir William recommended the factory be demolished and dismissed the Volkswagen Beetle as 'Too ugly, too noisy and unattractive to the private buyer'.

In 1949, Major Hirst and his team gave the Wolfsburg plant to the German government and the Lower Saxony regional authority. The Beetle went on to sell 23 million around the world during the next sixty-odd years, the sixth highest quantity of any car ever made. The first million had rolled off the assembly line by 1955, years before any British car would achieve that.

In contrast, the Rootes Group, struggling with its Hillman Imp, would start to be swallowed up by the American giant Chrysler during the 1960s and later disappear altogether amid mounting losses. Ironically, the success of the Beetle would help to hurt Chrysler in its own home market.

It wasn't until 1952, when British servicemen were returning from Germany with their unusual new motors, bought for a concessionary £100, that we saw our first Beetles on home shores. American servicemen, posted to Britain, liked them too and the first dealerships sprang up in Kent to meet the demand from RAF Manston, then a base for the US Air Force.

Volkswagen Motors Ltd came into being soon after, setting up its British HQ in Ramsgate and importing vehicles for many years through the town's royal harbour.

It's unlikely that any other car can claim to be the symbol of an entire popular culture. For large swathes of baby boomers taking to the roads in the 1960s, driving a Beetle – possibly hastily hand-painted in a range of psychedelic colours – was to refuse to conform and to stick up two fingers at the tired old establishment.

The Beetle's beginnings date from a darker age in 1930s Nazi Germany, when it was designed by Ferdinand Porsche to fulfil Adolf Hitler's plans for a people's car. A few had been built by 1938 but the Second World War put paid to the project.

Durable bodywork and a dependable air-cooled engine underpinned the Beetle, enabling it to offer unfussy comfort and performance in a distinctive shape during the decades that followed. Cult status reached its zenith in the flower power era, and the car's fame was further boosted by Walt Disney's six Herbie the Love Bug films. The star is a cream-painted Beetle decorated with racing stripes and the number 53.

At different times, convertible Beetles have been available but were always few and far between on British roads. Even battered Beetles could find a new lease of life as donors for kit-car projects or be turned into beach and dune buggies. Examples turn up at car shows and are worth admiring for their individuality.

Beetle production ceased in 1974 at Wolfsburg in the wake of the arrival of the Golf, Polo and Passat models, all of which helped to reverse Volkswagen's flagging fortunes. Other German plants carried on making the car until 1980. Manufacturing continued in Brazil and Mexico until 2003, where the Beetle had established itself as the car of choice for city taxis.

RARITY RATING

★★★★ UNMOLESTED 1950S AND '60S MODELS
★★★ ALL OTHER MODELS

Whitewall tyres contrast well with the colour of this late 1950s/early 1960s version of the Beetle.

AUSTIN-HEALEY 100 & 3000

1952–67

In the 1950s, buyers of British sports cars sought three main marques, MG, Triumph or Austin-Healey, and for the most part stayed loyal to them until they started a family and had to buy something more practical.

Probably the sexiest of the trio's offerings was the Austin-Healey 100, launched in the year when Princess Elizabeth became Queen. The car was unveiled at the 1952 Earls Court Motor Show (as the Healey Hundred) to wide acclaim. Such acclaim, in fact, that Leonard Lord, the powerful head of Austin, snapped up the marketing rights with Donald Healey over dinner one evening. By the time the show closed, the car was renamed the Austin-Healey 100 – 100 denoting its top speed.

Resplendent in red, with wire wheels, this Austin-Healey still cuts a dash more than sixty years after it rolled off the assembly line at Abingdon.

Bodies were built by Jensen at Wolverhampton before transfer to Austin's factories for final assembly.

The 100 was replaced at the end of the decade by the uprated, and often two-toned, Austin-Healey 3000, which had been given a power boost with a 2.9-litre, 124bhp (later 148bhp), straight-six engine and carried a price tag of £1,159. Additional stopping power was provided by disc brakes on the front wheels.

Quickly nicknamed the Big Healey, the motor enjoyed considerable competition success. Pat Moss, sister of F1 driver Stirling, drove it to an outright win in the 1960 Liege–Rome–

Many of the later Healeys were painted in two-tone colours – a fashionable extra during the late 1950s and early '60s.

Liege rally, while Big Healeys scored highly in Monte Carlo and the Alpine rallies of the early 1960s.

For many, the Big Healey was the last true British roadster and it is rightly revered today, the combination of power, sleek lines and sheer wind-in-the-hair fun marking it out from the common herd. It was replaced in 1967 by the less successful MGC.

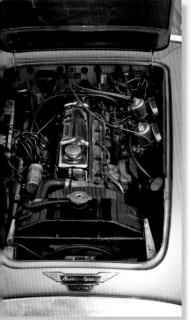

There is little spare room for spanners around this Austin-Healey's 3-litre engine.

> **RARITY RATING**
>
> ★★★★ ALL MODELS

DAIMLER CONQUEST

1953–58

Born with aristocratic looks, it was bred to be an owner driver's car by the Daimler Company – that is to say, you could give your chauffeur his P45 if you bought one!

Daimler was still a traditional company of craftsman-made cars – old fashioned and years behind the times, much like most of its customers, it could be said.

Launched in Queen Elizabeth II's coronation year for export only, the Conquest was an attempt by Daimler to move forward into the new Elizabethan age. The 2.5-litre engine, in early days mated to a four-speed pre-selector gearbox, eventually pushed this heavy car along to 70mph. Acceleration was as stately as the car's looks, so Daimler beefed up the performance on its Conquest Century in time for 1954. Century refers to bhp, by the way, not mph – this motor was flat out at 90mph.

I've seen only Conquest saloons on show – all in need of returning to their former glory. You may just be lucky enough to spot drophead coupé or roadster versions from time to time.

In spite of fast-rising star Norman Wisdom bringing celebrity endorsement to the Conquest when he bought a two-seater roadster in the early 1950s, it became clear to a more car-conscious public that it couldn't compete against the likes of the Jaguars of the day.

Daimler got the message too but not before losing sales after petrol rationing was introduced during the Suez crisis. Production finally ceased in early 1958 after some 10,000 examples of all types had been made. Around 300 are still with us, according to How Many Left?

The Conquest's walnut veneer fascia and centrally mounted dials have seen brighter days but still have style.

This Daimler Conquest was awaiting a new owner when seen at a classic car auction. Hopefully it went to a place where it would be given plenty of TLC. When new, the pre-purchase tax price was a hefty £1,066 – some say the car gets its name from this Battle of Hastings connection.

BORGWARD ISABELLA

1954–61

I confess I had never heard the name Borgward until chancing upon a pristine Isabella coupé parked up in the Sussex town of Petworth a few years ago – and I got a photo of it. An overheating problem had forced the owner to seek help from a local garage before he could continue his journey.

Safe to say, its handsome looks match its extreme rarity, particularly in right-hand-drive form.

The German Borgward company was run by Carl Friedrich Wilhelm Borgward, who spent his entire working life in the car industry. Before the Second World War he had built up a considerable business making lorries, a three-wheeler and the much-sought-after Hansa range of autos.

Spotted on the streets of Petworth, Sussex, this rare right-hand-drive Borgward Isabella stands out from modern cars.

He resumed car and lorry production in 1948 at his factory in Bremen and by June 1954 was able to unveil the first Isabellas – originally to be called Hansas, but the Isabella name used during development had stuck.

Isabellas slotted into the marketplace to match Mercedes for all-round quality but at a cheaper price. Fitted with an efficient 1500cc, four-cylinder engine, it could produce 75bhp, outperforming rivals and giving it sustained power for the autobahns.

The logical development of the saloon, far more sprightly than the lumbering 180 that was Mercedes's nearest match, was a sports coupé – in effect a grand tourer – and in 1957 Borgward introduced it.

The Isabella proved a commercial success through its relatively short life, selling more than 200,000 examples around the world. Borgward went bust in 1961, forcing the factory's closure a year later, by which time the parts stock had been used up. The site was sold to Mercedes-Benz, while many Borgward workers found new jobs with near neighbour BMW.

A thriving UK-based drivers' club reckons there are a few dozen Isabellas left on British roads today.

RARITY RATING

★★★★★ ALL MODELS

We're cheating a little here by showing a Borgward Isabella on display at a specialist show – but they are hard to find and this picture shows off the car's lines very well.

CITROËN DS

1955–75

Over the past century France has been responsible for some of the quirkiest-designed cars to take to the road but, of all of them, Citroën's DS surely wins the coconut for having some of the most outlandish looks.

Lined up for inspection at a classic car auction in Ashford, Kent, is this French-registered Citroën DS.

The smart interior of the DS is topped off by its single-spoked steering wheel.

At first sight, the DS looks like a beetle having a bad day (the insect, not the VW), but then looks often deceive. From its shark-nosed front end to the sloping back stance that makes you wonder how the rear wheels stay attached, the DS was highly aerodynamic for its time and packed with features like hydropneumatic suspension and disc brakes, not seen previously on mass-produced cars.

Thanks to the self-levelling suspension, the ride quality was ahead of its time, emphasising its technological superiority. Inside, a single-spoke steering wheel gave the car added design statement appeal.

When launched at the Paris Motor Show in 1955, it was an immediate hit with 12,000 ordered on the first day alone, a record that would only be broken by the Tesla Model 3 more than sixty years later.

The front-wheel-drive DS – pronounced as *déesse*, the French word for goddess – replaced the Traction Avant and was targeted at the executive market. Fans of the film *The Day of the Jackal* will spot several examples being shot at by crooks, including those forming a presidential motorcade.

For affluent Parisians the DS was the perfect vehicle to make the long journey every August for holidays in the south. An estate version known as the Safari arrived in 1959 for those with extra luggage and/or children to carry around.

During its twenty-year production run, some 1.5 million DSs were built, including a handful at Citroën's Slough factory for the British market. Today the few hundred remaining in the UK enjoy near-cult status and spotting one is a treat.

A portent of things to come for classic cars? This fully restored DS has been converted to run on electricity.

RARITY RATING

★★★★ SALOONS
★★★★★ SAFARIS

HILLMAN MINX

1956–67

Hillman, part of the Rootes Group, had been successfully selling its medium family saloons with the Minx name on them since the 1930s, but when the Series 1 arrived from Coventry in 1956, it represented a big move away from the earlier, and it has to be said dumpier, models of previous years.

Inspired by transatlantic trends for fins, big grilles and rakish rear angles, the Series 1 Minx was developed for the value-conscious motorist seeking something modern and reliable – but not necessarily technically advanced. The US influence is hardly surprising though, considering the Loewy Organisation, the styling house behind designs for Studebaker, came up with the shape of the Minx, code-named Audax during the planning stages.

Another transatlantic trend borrowed by Rootes was the annual upgrading – or tinkering, depending on your point of view – of the car.

The transatlantic styling influences of the Hillman Minx are evident in this two-tone example.

Front-end view of a Hillman Minx – note the twin driving lamps.

Bench front seat, centrally placed dials and a white steering wheel continue the American influences in the Minx interior.

The Series 1 was therefore followed by the Series 2 in 1957, the Series 3 in 1958, the 3a in 1959, the 3b in 1960 and the 3c in 1961. Series 5 and 6 appeared in 1963 and 1965 respectively (there was no Series 4).

Buyers could choose from a wide range of colours – some of them in flashy two-tone schemes – and engine sizes that grew over the years from 1400cc to 1700cc. Estate and much rarer convertible models were also offered. Singer Gazelle and Sunbeam Rapier variants offered more power and greater comfort for those with extra money to spare than the Minx's £795 asking price (which included £265 worth of purchase tax) in 1958.

Design-wise, the mid-1950s Minx could more than hold its own against contemporary motors from the likes of BMC, Vauxhall and Ford, but by the mid-1960s, its lines were looking tired and eventually it was replaced by a new Minx based on the Hillman Hunter.

According to How Many Left?, there are 1,000 Series 1–6 Minxes remaining on UK roads, while another 500 wait to be hauled out of their slumbers once again.

RARITY RATING

★★★★ SALOONS
★★★★★ ESTATES AND CONVERTIBLES

AUSTIN NASH METROPOLITAN

1957–61 (IN THE UK)

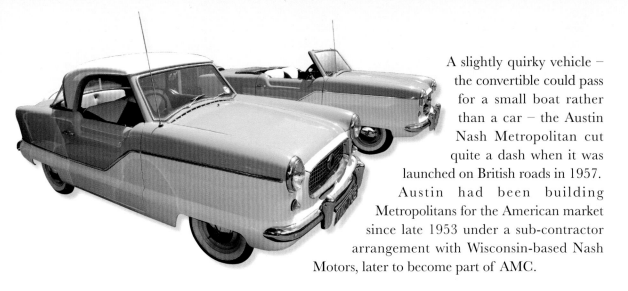

A slightly quirky vehicle – the convertible could pass for a small boat rather than a car – the Austin Nash Metropolitan cut quite a dash when it was launched on British roads in 1957. Austin had been building Metropolitans for the American market since late 1953 under a sub-contractor arrangement with Wisconsin-based Nash Motors, later to become part of AMC.

You wait years to spot an Austin Nash Metropolitan – and then two turn up at once. Belonging to the same east Kent-based owner since the 1990s are a 1958 convertible and a 1955 hard top. The latter was once owned by musician Phil Collins, to whom it was given as a wedding present by his then wife Jill Tavelman in 1984. The car had been sourced for her by their friend and fellow musician Robert Plant.

Under the bonnet of a 1950s Austin Nash Metropolitan.

The reconditioned seats of this Metropolitan are a credit to the trimmer, but the black parts would originally have been a houndstooth pattern.

Just as American cars were at the height of their bigger-is-better with fins and chrome era, the compact Metropolitan went against the trend. It proved quite a success, being marketed mainly at the growing number of women drivers across the States using it as a household's second vehicle.

Offered in hard- and open-top forms, with a selection of colourful two-tone finishes and bright interiors, the Metropolitan initially housed a 1.2-litre engine and three-speed gearbox – the mechanicals taken directly from Austin's proven A40 Counties range. It was easy to drive and cheap to run – two virtues highlighted by an early form of market research carried out by Nash among potential customers.

Ponderous steering and a large turning circle were the Metropolitan's main drawbacks, but it did come with a radio, electric wipers and heater as standard. The options of whitewall tyres and a spare-wheel cover mounted on the back end set off the overall look.

Austin built 104,000 of these cars between 1953 and 1961, with all but 9,000 meeting American demands. Only a few dozen are left on and off UK roads today – such is their rarity that the two examples shown here were the last cars to be photographed for this book and hadn't been to any shows for some time! They were tracked down to an east Kent owner who lives only 7 miles away from the author.

RARITY RATING

★★★★★ ALL MODELS

FIAT 500

1957–73

At the height of motoring's golden years of the 1950s, Germany had the Beetle, France the 2CV, Britain the Morris Minor and Italy the diminutive Fiat 500 to get people moving around their respective countries.

The little Fiat was launched in July 1957 as a town car, initially known as the Cinquecento. Standing at just on 9ft long and about 4ft wide, it was powered by a 479cc engine mounted at the back and, thanks to those dimensions, it qualified as a micro car. The car was built with two rear-hinged 'suicide doors' – to the delight of Italian men who liked seeing signoras' shapely legs as they climbed out. Years later, there would be many complaints when Fiat decided to hinge the doors at the front.

The Fiat 500's chic trendiness was all well and good in the sunnier climes of Rome, Turin or Milan, but perhaps not so obvious on a wet Thursday somewhere in the Home Counties. Seen here, from left, are the Fiat 500 Giardiniera estate, the saloon and its predecessor the Fiat Topolino, aka 'little mouse'.

If you weren't too tall, the 500 proved a versatile mover and met many social needs – first-time owners and drivers found them easy to handle, and they were ideal second cars for shopping and the school run for transporting your bambinos. City types liked to pose with them – especially the sporty models tuned to offer additional power.

Throughout the 1960s, a range of spin-offs was created. There is an estate version, the Giardiniera, which in right-hand drive is an extreme rarity on British roads. Italian tuning house Abarth got their hands on some 500s and turned them into pocket rockets, namely the 695ss. These can change hands now for tens of thousands of pounds.

By the time production ended in the mid-1970s, some 2.6 million 500s had rolled off the Turin production lines. Today, a thriving owners' club in Britain ensures Fiat 500s remain cherished. Not all stay on our roads, though. If you have about £8,500 to spare you can buy the front half of one that has been converted into a 100-litre fridge-freezer for your kitchen!

The Fiat 500 dashboard is spartan by modern standards but all the essentials for lights and wipers were easy to find.

Early Fiat 500s were fitted with rear-hinged 'suicide doors'.

RARITY RATING

★★★★ SALOONS
★★★★★ GIARDINIERA AND OTHER SPECIALS

PEERLESS GT 2 LITRE

1957–60

Spotting a 1958 phase-one Peerless GT 2 Litre at a local car show is rare indeed – perhaps not surprising when only 325 were built!

In the late 1950s Peerless Motors of Slough was a specialist making cars for enthusiasts and was set to prosper until defeat was snatched from the jaws of victory.

A Peerless GT could clock up 107mph, knocking spots off contemporary Triumph and Morgan rivals, with 0–60mph inside 13 seconds. A new Peerless would set you back £1,450, the accursed purchase tax accounting for £500.

To keep down costs, Peerless bodies were made of glass-reinforced plastic (GRP) – still a relatively new material for car-making in the 1950s – and fitted to a welded space frame chassis, mated with Triumph TR running gear.

In the late 1950s, the Peerless production line could only make five cars a week. A waiting list soon built up until extra GRP moulds arrived, enabling twenty-five a week to be made.

Successful hotelier James Byrne was an avid enthusiast who had wanted a car built to his own specifications. He had partnered with experienced engine builder Bernie Rodgers and eventually they launched the commercially viable 2+2 sports car in 1957.

John Gordon was appointed an additional director and success seemed assured when a Peerless finished sixteenth in the 1958 Le Mans twenty-four-hour race, winning its class. Orders arrived from America and selling 1,500 cars a year seemed possible.

Interior of a Peerless GT.

Frustratingly, the company directors fell out in 1959 and John Gordon resigned. Peerless declined further after Bernie Rodgers left and it folded two years later.

John Gordon teamed up with Jim Keeble to buy the remnants of Peerless and later build Gordon-Keeble cars, another rare sports marque.

RARITY RATING

★★★★★   ALL MODELS

ROVER P5

1958–73

If you watch 1960s and '70s news footage of prime ministers arriving at Downing Street when winning a general election or their minions resigning after owning up to dalliances with ladies of the night, there is a good chance their chauffeured ride would be in a Rover 3-litre, or P5.

The 3.5-litre coupé version of the Rover P5, denoted by the more angular rear roof line.

This solid and dependable car – which is more than can be said for some of its political passengers – was introduced by the Rover Company in 1958 to replace the venerated 100 and 101 series cars. The P5 had established itself as Whitehall's transport of choice within a couple of years and by the early 1970s the late Queen had treated herself to a green one as well.

Plenty of non-political heavyweights bought this powerful and well-appointed vehicle too and by the time the Mk2 came on the market in 1962, some 21,000 had been sold. The Mk2 model saw its power plant tweaked to give 129hp, better suspension and quarter-light windows.

For the first time there was a coupé version, easily recognised by its angular rear window and roof line. It also came with power steering as standard.

It wasn't until the fourth and final version, the P5B, arrived in 1967 that it received an extra 500cc. It used the Buick-inspired V8 aluminium engine, which would haul countless Rovers around for years afterwards – as well as MGB GTs, thanks to BMC ownership of both companies. This engine offered 158bhp of power and drank a gallon of petrol every 22 or 23 miles.

By the time production came to an end in 1973, some 60,000 saloons and coupés had been built, the last batch being snapped up by our government for more ministerial cruising and lasting long enough for James Callaghan and Margaret Thatcher to enjoy their comfort. Today, about 1,400 examples survive on and off our roads.

The Rover P5's cockpit smacked of spare-no-expense quality.

Ministerial *derrières* could be sure of a comfortable journey in the back of the P5.

> ## RARITY RATING
>
> ★★★★   ALL MODELS

DAIMLER DART SP250

1959–64

Bespoke limousine builder Daimler very much broke its own mould when announcing the convertible Dart SP250 back in 1959. Built in Coventry, it would be the last true Daimler as the company was sold to Jaguar the following year.

Unveiled in New York in April 1959, it was unofficially named the ugliest car of the show, while US rival Chrysler, who owned the Dart trademark, threatened legal action if the name wasn't changed. Hence, Daimler's new baby became the SP250 after its project number during development – but the Dart name didn't go away.

Powered by a 2.5-litre V8 engine, the body was made of fibreglass, chosen to hasten the car into production and considerably cheaper than fabricating steel pressings.

Daimler intended to sell 3,000 SP250s a year, mostly Stateside and, to keep the price down, offered it as a no-frills motor with a long list of options to negate import duties. Fog lights, heaters, seatbelts and even bumpers were among the tax-beating add-ons.

The Metropolitan Police bought two black SP250s in 1961, the first time the capital's coppers had acquired sports cars for patrol use, and eventually bought another twenty-four during the next three years.

Spotted on display in east Kent, this Daimler Dart cuts a dash just standing still.

Under the bonnet of an SP250. (© Brightwells)

The rozzers intended their cars to be used to 'encourage courtesy on the roads' – in reality they were used for nicking errant biker boys, mainly where the North Circular Road met the A1 and M1. So it was that many young people's first encounter of this remarkable sports car was in their rear-view mirror – complete with ringing Winkworth bell and a flashing blue light. Other police forces realised the SP250's potential and bought them, particularly for patrolling the new motorways.

Sales were never high and by the time Jaguar halted production to avoid competition with its new E-type, some 2,656 had been built. How Many Left? suggests that nearly 700 are in the UK, with around 100 awaiting their return to the road.

RARITY RATING

★★★★ ALL MODELS

A lovingly preserved SP250, the handset and radio on the passenger side telling us this car was once used by the police 'to encourage courtesy on the roads'.

FORD ANGLIA

1959–67

To Harry Potter fans, this car is instantly recognisable; to the rest of us, it's the distinctive Ford Anglia 105E.

Ford had already been using the Anglia name for some years on its austerity-era 'sit up and beg' models by the time this transatlantic-influenced replacement started rolling off the Dagenham assembly lines in late 1959. The Anglia's reverse-sloped rear window helped set it apart from anything else on British roads – in the rain, the glass stayed dry and clear.

Anglia's launch price was £610 and you got a four-speed gearbox – a first for British Fords – mated to a lively 'Kent' four-cylinder,

Surviving Anglias are counted in the lower hundreds today. Some spare parts can be hard to trace, especially the front bumper, which is common to Lotus Elans and Europas – making them expensive when they do surface on the market.

997cc, crossflow engine. Like many motors of the day, carpets and radios were extras, so accommodation in the basic Anglia could be a little spartan – if you splashed out for the Deluxe model, a heater and windscreen washers were part of the deal. Buyers couldn't get enough of the Anglia and the car went on to become Ford of Britain's first million seller.

Van and estate versions were added in 1961 but few have survived. An upmarket 123E Super saloon was launched in 1962, denoted by its range of two-tone colour schemes and chrome hubcaps. The Anglia was among the first cars to get metallic paint – choices of Venetian Gold and Blue Mink were offered. Under the bonnet there was a 1198cc engine, capable of pulling the car to 90mph.

Ford produced Anglias until 1967, by which time it had made 1,083,000 of them, of which some 100,000 were estates. The Anglia was replaced by Ford's next bestseller, the Escort.

The interior of the Anglia Deluxe. (© Brightwells)

The Anglia's reverse-sloped back window was meant to help keep rain off the glass.

RARITY RATING

★★★ SALOONS
★★★★ ESTATES AND VANS

JAGUAR MK2

1959–67

Bank robbers and wage snatchers made the Jaguar Mk2 the getaway car of choice whenever they went blagging. Happily, the police bought them as well to give themselves an even chance of nicking them afterwards.

During the 1960s, in London at least, police were instructed to pull over any Jaguar Mk2 they saw with two or more people inside lest they be criminals planning their next job.

None of this cops-and-robbers stuff is what Sir William Lyons, head of Jaguar, would have had in mind when his company launched the Mk2 in 1959. Far from it: the Mk2 was designed to appeal to well-heeled professional types who liked comfort with speed and whose only doubtful behaviour might be to fiddle their expenses or fall in love with someone else's wife.

Badge engineering at its finest – the Daimler equivalent of the Jaguar Mk2 offered luxury with exclusivity.

Looking resplendent in resale red, this Mk2 has clearly been well cared for.

There's almost enough wood used in the Jaguar fascia to make a sideboard for your granny's dining room!

Offered with a 3.4-litre engine, these were powerful cars but a lot safer to drive than forebears produced earlier in the decade – F1 champion Mike Hawthorn died in his 1955 Jaguar after losing control of it on the Hog's Back in Surrey. Disc brakes all round, a wider rear track and a wrap-around rear window to improve vision helped make the Mk2 a more balanced motor.

A 3.8-litre model followed for 1960 (along with a Daimler version), to ensure the leaping cat stayed ahead of the pack – with a maximum speed of 125mph on tap, it could leave many other compact sports cars in its wake and would help to turn heads until the Mk2 moved over in 1967 for the more budget-conscious, yet stylistically unchanged, 240 and 340 models.

According to How Many Left?, around 1,500 to 2,000 of the original 80,000 built remain on or off our roads for us to admire today.

RARITY RATING

★★★★ ALL MODELS, INCLUDING DAIMLERS

AUSTIN MINI/MORRIS MINI-MINOR/THE MINI

1959–2000

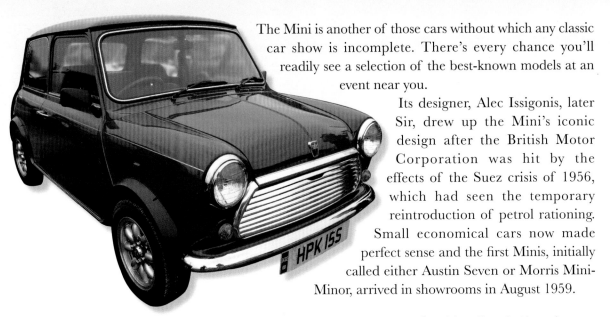

The Mini is another of those cars without which any classic car show is incomplete. There's every chance you'll readily see a selection of the best-known models at an event near you.

Its designer, Alec Issigonis, later Sir, drew up the Mini's iconic design after the British Motor Corporation was hit by the effects of the Suez crisis of 1956, which had seen the temporary reintroduction of petrol rationing. Small economical cars now made perfect sense and the first Minis, initially called either Austin Seven or Morris Mini-Minor, arrived in showrooms in August 1959.

Although modified with more recent flourishes like plastic arches, this Mini traces its origins back to the late 1970s.

A line-up of classic Minis from the 1970s to the '90s.

The Mini was kitted out with a transverse-mounted – that's sideways on, to you – 850cc engine driving the front wheels. The suspension was set up using rubber cones while the side windows slid horizontally to open. This allowed door pockets to be fitted as part of the overall generous amount of internal storage.

Rivals Ford quietly bought a Mini themselves and took it completely to pieces, trying in vain to figure out how a profit could be made when being sold for just shy of £500. Ford estimated BMC was losing about £30 on each car and a director even phoned BMC to tell them! On this basis, Ford chose to stay away from making small cars and concentrate on building medium saloons, a decision that paved the way for the best-selling Escort and Cortina models.

This 1967 Mini has been given a new lease of life since its engine was replaced with an all-electric drivetrain.

The original Mini offered a neat but basic layout in the cockpit.

BMC might not have made much money on the Mini but its influence on the British and international car markets cannot be underestimated. The Mini is one of the most revolutionary cars ever made, standing alongside the Ford Model T and the Volkswagen Beetle in bringing cheap transport to the masses.

Minis were slow to catch on and it wasn't until the souped-up Coopers won Monte Carlo rallies in the early 1960s and celebrities started buying them as runabouts that they began to sell in big numbers. Actor Peter Sellers famously ordered a coach-built Hooper Mini in 1962, sprayed purple with a basket-weave pattern on both doors.

The Mini became as much a part of the decadent 1960s as miniskirts, and its place in the British motoring psyche was assured when it stole the show in the 1969 film *The Italian Job* from stars Michael Caine and Noël Coward. Cult status has stayed with the Mini ever since.

Its basic design wouldn't change greatly, other than squaring off the front end to create the Clubman versions during the 1970s and adding better interior equipment.

Complete with roof rack, the half-timbered Mini Countryman of the 1960s brought a quality look to the range. Just make sure the wood is well cared for!

The Riley Elf, complete with a traditional front grille and a bustle boot, was a much plusher version of the Mini.

By the time production ended at Longbridge in October 2000, some 5.3 million Minis had been made and sold worldwide. Look out for the rarer variants of the Mini – an original pace-setting Cooper S is so highly prized it warrants a security guard when on public display! Canvas-topped pick-ups and vans are hard to come by, as is the Moke, an attempt at a military Mini.

Estate versions of all eras are few and far between too, particularly the half-timbered Countryman models, with good examples changing hands for between £15,000 and £18,000. The 1960s Wolseley Hornet and the Riley Elf were the posher saloons, featuring bustle-style boots, leather seats, veneer fascia and 998cc engines.

Germany's BMW took over the MG Rover company, the brand's then owner, in 1994 and unveiled its bulkier breed of Mini in Paris during autumn 2000. To date, it has sold nearly 4 million of them.

RARITY RATING

★★ UNMOLESTED 1980S STANDARD MODELS AND LIMITED EDITIONS BUILT BEFORE 1990

★★★ UNMOLESTED STANDARD 1960S AND '70S MODELS

★★★★ ESTATE, PICK-UP, VAN, CLUBMAN, MOKE, HORNET AND ELF VARIANTS

★★★★★ ORIGINAL-SPEC 1960S COOPER AND COOPER S MODELS

MORRIS OXFORD &
AUSTIN CAMBRIDGE

1959–71

There's a tale from the mid-1950s that the then Duke of Edinburgh, while touring BMC's Longbridge factory with its chief Sir Leonard Lord, allegedly criticised the company's designs for being dull when compared to its rivals. In fairness, the duke was correct; BMC in the 1950s was characterised by small bulbous cars that seemed to wheeze at the slightest effort.

The mainstay of the Farina-designed BMC range was the Austin Cambridge, this being a well-kept early 1960s example.

Lord was so stung by his remarks that he phoned Italian design studio Pinin Farina the day after the royal visit to come up with some ideas for flashy new motors, including a family saloon.

The result of all that was the heavily badge-engineered range of finned Farinas, better known to everyday folk as the Morris Oxford and the Austin Cambridge. Those willing to put up a bit more cash could opt for glammed-up versions wearing the revered Riley, Wolseley or MG names fore and aft.

Inside the Riley 4/72 – leather and wood feature strongly.

The Wolseley 15/60 was the first to be unveiled in 1959, quickly followed by the Cambridge and Riley models. Among the common features of the cars was the 1489cc B-series engine, a slightly detuned version of what was fitted to MGBs. Parts for these engines are still easy to come by thanks to the MG spares trade today.

The Oxford and Cambridge brought conservative family motoring to the respectable middle classes and, with estate versions arriving in the early 1960s, proved a mainstay of the decade's transport alongside the rival Ford Cortina.

Facelifted with slightly slimmer tail fins in 1961, the Oxford and Cambridge names were swapped for the Mk6 and A60 respectively. A diesel version was launched too, the only British-made car like this at the time, sold mainly to the private-hire trade.

At today's car shows, look out for the Austin Westminster and Van Den Plas Princess six-cylinder engine variants too, the latter being a 4-litre supplied by Rolls-Royce. Aimed at the executive market of their day, both vehicles were lavishly equipped with deep carpets, a radio, a wooden fascia and leather seats.

Past their best by the late 1970s, many Farinas faced an ignominious end on Britain's banger-racing circuits so survivors are relatively few, about 2,000 all told.

The imposing grille of the Wolseley 16/60, complete with light-up emblem in the centre.

RARITY RATING

★★★   OXFORD & CAMBRIDGE SALOONS
★★★★ ALL OTHERS, INCLUDING ESTATES

TRIUMPH HERALD

1959–71

Among the bumper crop of new cars launched in Britain during 1959 was the Triumph Herald. By the end of that year it was competing with the Mini, Ford Anglia, Austin A40 – and holding its own both in sales and on the roads.

Created by then relative unknown Italian designer Giovanni Michelotti – he had actually been the brains behind styling Ferraris – the Herald was not overly advanced for the time. The car stuck to being made from a separate body and chassis. Truth was owners Standard-Triumph couldn't afford the tooling for the newer monocoque process. Its 948cc engine was carried across from the obsolete Standard 10 until larger 1200cc and 1300cc ones took over a couple of years later.

A two-tone-painted Herald was a pretty car with rear fins and more than a little chrome on the front. It was easy to handle, as proved by countless driving schools buying them for their learners, and at £702 when launched, it wasn't beyond too many pockets.

The Herald was the first British car to have all-round independent suspension.

Still going strong – a late Herald estate spotted at the kerbside.

With the bonnet swung forward, a Herald's front wheel made a comfy perch to sit upon while having a tea break from maintenance duties.

Heralds were built in two- and four-door saloon and estate forms, along with a now rare two-seater coupé. In 1962, the Vitesse emerged offering greater performance through a 1600cc, six-cylinder engine – later this would be ramped up to 2000cc. Four headlights ensured you could see better at night. A convertible model was offered as well.

If you had to work on your Herald, the one-piece bonnet and wings opened forward, leaving the entire engine bay, wheels and suspension readily accessible.

Today, about 4,300 Heralds and Vitesses remain on and off our roads, according to figures on the How Many Left? website.

RARITY RATING

★★★ SALOONS
★★★★ ESTATES AND VANS
★★★★★ COUPÉS AND CONVERTIBLES

JAGUAR E-TYPE

1961–73

Famously described by Enzo Ferrari as the most beautiful car in the world soon after its Geneva launch in March 1961, the Jaguar E-Type took the world by storm.

Its long, low, sleek looks, combined with huge power to push it past 140mph, ensured the E-Type soon earned a high place in the annals of motoring history.

You may be a little hard-pressed to see one in the metal at a classic car show near you – the more specialist events are better places to find them – not because they are especially rare but because of their stellar value. With even ropey ones in need of work changing hands for at least £40,000, the really prime examples warrant a security guard either side of them if they are on display!

The E-type was offered as a drophead roadster as well as closed coupé. The earliest examples, with 3.8-litre engines, are the most collectable, but the last-of-the-line 5.3-litre V12s produced in the early 1970s – when British Leyland was running Jaguar and couldn't give them away – have gained in popularity during recent years.

The impressive frontage of an early 1970s series 3 Jaguar E-Type.

For many, the E-Type to really cherish is the Series 2 model. Upgraded from 1964 with a 4.2-litre power plant, it boasted a smoother gearbox, better brakes and more comfortable seats. Even these beauties were messed around with for the important American market by detuning the engines and sticking on heftier bumpers.

Demand for RHD E-Types outstrips supply today, and a growing number have been repatriated from the US to be converted on these shores to feed that market. Many have come from the sunshine states like California, where rust has been less likely to take its toll.

Shapes of front grilles and whether or not the lights are covered in denote externally some of the differences between the three series of E-Type. About 7,800 survive on and off our roads in 2022, according to How Many Left? All are a special treat to see, though.

Rocker switches for every occasion fill the dash of the E-Type.

A spotless V12 engine powers this immaculately restored example.

RARITY RATING

★★★★ ALL MODELS

RENAULT 4

1961–94

It may have taken French Renault a dozen years to respond to arch-rival Citroën's 2CV but the Renault 4 – or Quatrelle – was worth the wait, arriving in 1961 when the Gallic economy was on the up.

If the 2CV is as Gallic as a beret-wearing onion seller, then the Renault 4 ranks in the national identity with can-can dancers of the Folies Bergère. The 4 sold a million globally in its first five years, proving to be a clever balance between comfort, economy and contemporary style.

Powered by a 747cc, water-cooled engine, it was Renault's first front-wheel-drive car and kitted with independent suspension and rack-and-pinion steering.

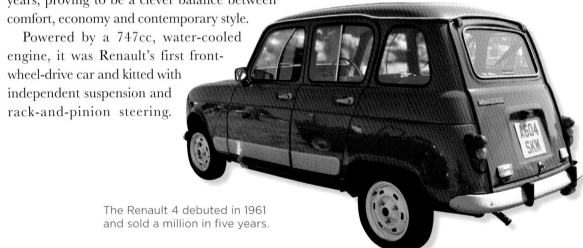

The Renault 4 debuted in 1961 and sold a million in five years.

The van version proved as much a sales hit as the saloon. Some models were fitted with a giraffe-style hatch door at the rear.

It was a more up-to-date take on the 2CV's appeal as a cheap, do-almost-anything kind of motor, able to take a beating across ploughed fields as well as battlefields; the French Army showed interest in a 4x4 version but didn't follow up on the idea. A van model featured a high-cube rear behind the cab and, with a giraffe-style hatch door, it proved a big hit with French bread stick makers and the postal service.

By the end of the 1970s, the 4 had been given a power boost with a 1100cc engine, as used in the Renault 6, to help it keep up with growing traffic levels. When production ceased – the last ones were made in Morocco and Slovenia – the car had outlived many of its contemporaries with 8,135,000 eventually sold around the world.

Plenty of 4s found their way on to Britain's roads, being built, if not in France, in the Republic of Ireland, including a number of special editions that only add to the car's rarity today. How Many Left? suggests that fewer than 300 are in road-going order, with a similar number on SORN.

RARITY RATING

★★★★ ALL MODELS

VOLVO P1800

1961-72

Sporty and Swedish aren't usually words used in the same sentence when describing cars, but the Volvo P1800 is probably the exception.

It's not as Swedish as you might think, though. There was a lot of British input into the P1800 – quite apart from it becoming famous as the transport of choice for Roger Moore playing The Saint in the 1960s TV series.

Volvo had come up with a design by the end of the 1950s for its well-appointed and sporty motor but had nowhere to build it as the Gothenburg production lines were busy turning out other models.

Thanks to Roger Moore's Simon Templar, every Volvo P1800 has to be white!

A deal was done with the Pressed Steel Company – which built car bodies for several makers – to stamp out the shells at Linwood, near Glasgow, the same place where Hillman Imps were fabricated. P1800 bodies would then be ferried south to West Bromwich for final assembly at Jensen's factory.

Rear emblem detail.

Unfortunately, quality-control standards weren't what the Swedes desired and after 6,000 had been built in Britain, Volvo found space in Gothenburg to build its renamed P1800S there.

Right-hand-drive cars first appeared in Britain during 1963, two years after the European launch, and came equipped with overdrive as standard, along with twin carbs and disc brakes at the front. Priced around £1,850, it was targeted at the higher end of the market alongside Rover and Jaguar. It offered a comfortable drive and could just make it past the ton but suffered – or their drivers did – with heavy steering. Looks-wise, though, it was and is a stunner.

Don't expect to see P1800s at every car show. Of the 40,000 built, around 300 remained in Britain by 2022, with just two automatics, according to How Many Left? Encouragingly, figures suggest more P1800s are being restored as people realise their classic potential.

RARITY RATING

★★★★ ALL MODELS WITH
MANUAL GEARBOX
★★★★★ AUTOMATIC MODELS

The Volvo P1800's interior, as penned by the Ghia and Frua design studios. Note the dash-mounted interior mirror.

AUSTIN/MORRIS 1100 & 1300

1962–73

A comparatively rare sight now, the Austin 1100, along with its badge-engineered siblings, was the most popular choice to keep 1960s Britain moving.

It was known by its design office project tag ADO16 and masterminded by Sir Alec Issigonis, fresh from his success with the Mini. The British Motor Corporation launched the first variant, the Morris 1100, in 1962, while cars bearing the Austin badge wouldn't arrive until the following year. The slightly more powerful 1300s didn't reach the showrooms until 1967.

For its time, the 1100 was an advanced small motor, appealing across the car-buying spectrum from first-time owners to small families. Its ease of handling also made it popular with irritatingly slow older drivers forever on their way to the bowls club, the Masonic Lodge or the Women's Institute!

The front grille of the Wolseley 1300. The winged badge would be illuminated with the side lights.

The MG version of the ADO16 is one of the hardest versions of the range to find. This late 1960s model would have had more urgency than some thanks to twin carburettors feeding fuel to its engine.

Under the bonnet of a Morris 1100, which has plenty of patina.

An Austin 1100 Super de Luxe model from 1968 and first registered in Leicester.

Disc brakes were fitted at the front for better stopping power, while the all-new fluid-based Hydrolastic suspension offered a remarkably smooth ride. BMC's trusted transverse-mounted A-series engine provided the power to the front wheels. As a result, just as in the Mini, the cabin was generous, if not a little basic.

That could be remedied by ordering one of the plusher versions of the car. The 1100 series would become the most badge-engineered car of all time. In the years following, features including leather seats, walnut veneer fascia, rev counters, picnic tables, thicker carpets, fog lights and reversing lights found their way on to the Riley Kestrel, the MG 1100 (and 1300), the Wolseley 1300 and the Van Den Plas versions, complete with their own styled front ends and grilles to differentiate them from the common herd. A second carburettor in the MG, Wolseley and VDP models gave the engine a few extra horses but overall, while performance wasn't sluggish, it wasn't going to set the world on fire either.

Things took a turn for the better in the early 1970s when the sporty 1300 GT arrived to give the tired marque a much-needed lift and it's these models, often painted orange with a vinyl roof, that are the most sought after now.

Famously, the capacious Countryman – or estate – made its mark on millions of fans of the BBC's 1970s *Fawlty Towers* sitcom when John Cleese's raging Basil Fawlty thrashes his car with the branch of a nearby tree after it has broken down at a time of crisis.

The 1100 and 1300 would be a familiar sight on our roads years after production finished in 1973. However, many met an inglorious end after failing the MOT test because the sub-frame – the structural component holding the front suspension and engine in place – was rusting beyond redemption.

Not exactly brimming with extras in the cabin, the 1100 interior was functional but well laid out – and there was a heater to warm up colder journeys.

In all, some 2 million of these motors were eventually made. They topped the sales charts for a number of years in the 1960s but near the end symbolised the downward spiral that strike-hit British Leyland was taking – a situation worsened only by the debut of its replacement, the Austin Allegro.

RARITY RATING

★★★★ AUSTIN & MORRIS 1100 & 1300 SALOONS

★★★★★ ALL OTHER MODELS, ESPECIALLY ESTATES, WOLSELEYS AND RILEY KESTRELS

MGB ROADSTER & GT

1962–80

No respectable classic car show is complete without a clutch of at least half a dozen MGB roadsters or GTs.

Possibly the most common of British classic cars – there are about 38,000 MGBs on and off Britain's roads now, according to How Many Left? – they are among the most endearing.

The convertible roadsters were first off MG's Abingdon production line in 1962, powered by 1800cc, four-cylinder engines. The hatchback Pinin Farina-designed GTs followed three years later, offering back-seat space – for dogs, children and the vertically challenged at any rate – for the first time.

Think of an archetypal small sports car and the chances are you will quickly think of a top-down, wind-in-the-hair MGB.

Some 80 per cent of MGBs were exported to the USA. Ever-tighter safety regulations introduced there in the mid-1970s forced the change to clunky-looking rubber bumpers in place of chrome ones.

Today's Euroboxes will easily leave MGBs behind at the lights but at least you travel with a certain panache. Not for nothing was the MGB GT dubbed the 'poor man's Aston Martin'.

Under the bonnet of the 3.5-litre V8 model. This is an early one dating from 1973.

Some half a million MGBs had been built by the time cash-strapped British Leyland closed the factory in October 1980 – seen by many as a shameful act of corporate vandalism.

The earliest versions produced until the late 1960s are arguably the most sought after, but anything produced before autumn 1974 with chrome bumpers (and ideally wire wheels as well) will always be preferred to the later rubber-bumper models. That said, so many later cars have been converted to sport chrome, rubber-bumper versions are becoming scarce!

Although every MGB is now at least forty years old, they enjoy a strong global following. Owners clubs and an industry supplying copious replacement parts make restorations viable.

Look out also for the B's powerful sisters, the 2.5-litre, six-cylinder MGC, easily spotted by its humped bonnet, and the 3-litre MGB V8. The latter was introduced in 1973, just as an oil crisis hit the UK, and its relative thirstiness proved its undoing.

RARITY RATING

★ MGB ROADSTER
★★ GT
★★★ MGC AND MGB V8

The author's own classic car is a 1973 example of the MGB GT.

TRIUMPH SPITFIRE & GT6

1962–80

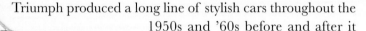

Triumph produced a long line of stylish cars throughout the 1950s and '60s before and after it became part of BMC. They were designed mainly by Giovanni Michelotti, and have become highly regarded classics today. Among them is the Triumph Spitfire, a strong rival for MG's Midget and Austin Healey-Sprite, which was launched at the Earls Court Motor Show in October 1962. Its striking looks helped build a firm following, particularly among the growing number of female buyers taking to the roads for the first time.

The 1960s examples of the Triumph Spitfire had a more rounded look to them than '70s versions.

Ready for some roof-down fun in a later Triumph Spitfire.

By the end of the 1970s, Spitfires were more tapered at their rear ends with lights and number plate being given a corporate style in common with larger Triumph cars.

The curvaceous design stayed recognisably the same throughout the Spitfire's long life but did see revisions to front and back ends. Bumpers were raised and rubberised by the 1970s to fall in line with fast-changing US regulations. Somehow Triumph designers made a better fist of this than their British Leyland colleagues at MG.

Early Spitfires looked fast but weren't really quick as they had the same 1200cc engines 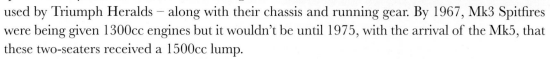 used by Triumph Heralds – along with their chassis and running gear. By 1967, Mk3 Spitfires were being given 1300cc engines but it wouldn't be until 1975, with the arrival of the Mk5, that these two-seaters received a 1500cc lump.

Targeting the same market as buyers of the coupé MGB GT was the Spitfire's saucy sister, the Triumph GT6. With its sexy, sloping roofline, you would be forgiven for thinking this was merely a fastback version of the Spitfire. But no, the GT6 had been ramped up with the 2-litre, straight-six power plant out of the company's 2000 saloon. Apparently, the weight of the roof considerably hampered the smaller 1200cc engine.

Offered in three distinct versions between 1966 and 1973, some 41,000 GT6s were made, about one-fifth of the final number of Spitfires. In 2022, around 8,700 Spitfires survive on and off road in the UK along with 1,900 GT6s.

RARITY RATING

★★★ TRIUMPH SPITFIRE
★★★★ TRIUMPH GT6

HILLMAN IMP

1963–76

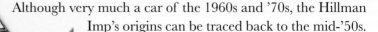

Although very much a car of the 1960s and '70s, the Hillman Imp's origins can be traced back to the mid-'50s. The Rootes Group, which owned Hillman, was well known for its middle and upmarket cars but had nothing in the small-car sector – a market growing fast since the 1956 Suez crisis and petrol rationing.

Development had seen the difficult birth of a project car called Slug, but the resulting return to the drawing board brought forth a more refined vehicle using a superb 875cc, and later 925cc, Coventry Climax aluminium engine mounted, unusually in the UK, at the rear.

A well-cared-for example of a 1970 Hillman Imp, impressive in red, and originally registered in Glamorgan, South Wales.

Building the Imp required a new factory but government pressure led Rootes, unwillingly, to site its new plant at Linwood near Glasgow, well away from its heartland in Coventry.

Had the Imp arrived a few years earlier, it could have been a scene-stealer against the Mini, Ford Anglia or Triumph Herald, but the project overran and the Imp was late to the party. Desperate to get the car launched, production began before some features were fully proved.

A rare example of the van version, known as the Commer Imp. The first ones arrived in late 1965. In all, some 18,000 were built in a four-year-long production run. (David Lodge)

The higher-spec Singer Chamois appeared a year after the Imp's launch.

Other factors loomed large in the model's undoing. Despite huge investment in Scotland, engine blocks were still being machined in the Midlands. The Scottish workforce was inexperienced at assembling cars – perhaps more used to the heavier metal-bashing work of shipbuilding – and industrial relations were at a low ebb.

What should have been an excellent little car quickly got a reputation for unreliability and poor performance. By the time the faults had been ironed out, the Imp name was a tarnished one.

A year after the first Imps appeared, the more luxurious Singer Chamois arrived. A square-backed estate version, called the Hillman Husky, followed and by the end of the 1960s buyers could opt for a sporty-looking Sunbeam Stiletto as well, distinguished by its fastback styling.

Close to 500,000 Imps were made and today it's the Stiletto that is most sought after, but all versions are proving hard to find. How Many Left? suggests fewer than 800 were on UK roads in late 2022, with another 600 awaiting revival.

RARITY RATING

★★★★★ ALL MODELS INCLUDING VANS.
THE BASIC MODEL IS RAREST TO SPOT

LOTUS EUROPA S1 & S2

1966–75

For most of us, the nearest we got to seeing one of these low, ground-hugging motors was the Matchbox toy version. Imagine my surprise when, in the early 1970s, I learned someone in my village had acquired a real Lotus Europa!

The Norfolk-made Europa developed from Lotus's bid for Ford's GT40 racing project in 1963. When the contract went elsewhere, Lotus boss Colin Chapman took the idea as a basis for a new mid-engined roadgoing car, replacing the Lotus 7.

Lotus eschewed the Ford componentry it had relied upon for earlier cars and replaced it with the modern running gear in the newly launched, but rather sedate, Renault 16. Positioning, retuning and rotation of its engine and back axle gave Lotus the ideal mid-engine set-up it sought – but offered four reverse gears. Some nifty work in the differential assembly soon corrected this aberration.

The angle of this photo emphasises the low profile of the Lotus Europa, this example being a limited-edition model from 1973, marking success on the track that year.

The engine block itself, made partly from aluminium, kept the car's weight down, while the ancillaries now faced rearwards, giving easy access for maintenance.

The Europa Series 1 was announced to the world in late 1966, with first deliveries the following year. The Series 1 would prove the rarer of the two versions as only 296 were built.

The Series 2 was launched in April 1968, still using the same Renault running gear but other refinements included electric windows and adjustable seats. Three years later, a twin-cam version, powered by the Lotus-Ford 105bhp racing engine, made its debut. When the Lotus F1 racing team won the world championship in 1972, a limited edition Europa was produced in sponsor John Player Special colours. The special element of the name was retained until the end of Europa production in 1975, by which time 4,300 Series 2s had been made. Around 500 Europas are thought to be on and off British roads today, according to How Many Left?

The cockpit of the Lotus Europa.

RARITY RATING

★★★★★ ALL MODELS

ROVER 2000 P6

1963–77

The Rover
P6 exudes
solidity and robustness
through its curving lines.

For decades, the Rover Company of Solihull had produced solid-looking cars for bank managers, country solicitors and other paid-up members of the middle classes with which to maintain their social standing as well as cruising around in.

That radically changed in 1963 with the arrival of the Rover 2000, officially known as the P6, when it was launched to critical acclaim and became the first ever winner of the coveted European Car of the Year award.

Beneath sleek, futuristic styling was a strong base unit 'cage' to which all the outer panels were affixed, giving the car tremendous strength and rigidity. Internally, the car was finished to a high standard with a great deal of thought given to reducing injuries in an accident.

It wasn't only the well-heeled Rover customer base who bought these cars. The 2-litre engine appealed to younger, junior management types keen to establish their credentials without graduating to a more starchy-looking gas guzzler.

A twin-carb version of the 2 litre, designated TC, was introduced in 1966; originally Rover had said it wouldn't bother with this as the recent introduction of Britain's blanket 70mph speed limit made it superfluous. Single-carburettor engines were still available and labelled as SC models.

The P6 3.5-litre V8 arrived in April 1968 after Rover's new owner, British Leyland, bought the rights to the aluminium engine from Buick, giving the car a 0–60 time of 10.5 seconds and a maximum speed of 114mph. The V8 could more than hold its own against other cars in its class, perhaps with the exception of the Jaguar 3.4.

Production of the P6 continued until early 1977, by which time about 350,000 had been built. How Many Left? estimates 1,200 2000s survive, with a further 1,100 3.5 V8s on and off our roads.

For its time, the Rover P6 – a 2000 is shown here – boasted a well-equipped interior that included a clock in the centre of the dashboard.

RARITY RATING

★★★   ALL MODELS

VAUXHALL VIVA HA

1963-66

Life was short for the HA version of the Vauxhall Viva as it had a production span of only three years. But in that time it helped Vauxhall establish itself as a serious manufacturer of compact family cars – which was borne out by its HB and HC successors.

My judgement of the HA is clouded by my childhood travels with family. Journeys to school or faraway holiday expeditions meant enduring the cramped position of sitting in the back of two examples, both painted cream as it happens.

The Vauxhall Viva HA made its debut in 1963 and was the company's first foray into the small-car market.

One was bought brand new in 1966 and gave generally reliable service for the following six years, the other was acquired second-hand and meant my mum had her own set of wheels at last.

The Viva was designed mainly for women drivers – now a viable market segment as thousands were passing their tests throughout the decade – and young families.

The neat dashboard of the Viva with fuel gauge, oil and ignition lights in one dial.

Based around Vauxhall's German GM counterpart, the Opel Kadett, the Viva HA was built both in Luton and in a purpose-built plant at Ellesmere Port on Merseyside, the latter commencing assembly of HAs in June 1964. Some 100,000 cars were built there in the first ten months. By the time HA production ended, that number had trebled.

The HA delivered cheap motoring to many in its £566 no-frills form. For a few pounds extra you could have disc brakes on the front wheels as well.

Although replaced after three years, the HA lived on, its front end retained for the van version, latterly known as the Bedford Beagle, which proved a mainstay of the British Telecom, British Rail and British Gas engineers' fleets of the 1970s and '80s. A few Beagles were converted by Dormobile into compact camper vans.

Funnily enough, our family 1966 HA survived until sometime in the late 1970s!

Under the HA's bonnet.

RARITY RATING

★★★★ SALOONS
★★★★★ VANS

JENSEN INTERCEPTOR

1966–76

Its very name suggests a galactic vessel ready for a showdown with the starship *Enterprise*. In reality, this was a high-performance grand tourer hand-assembled in West Bromwich.

Interceptors were instantly desirable cars when launched in 1966 with their mix of American Chrysler 6-litre V8 engines and Italian styling by Carrozzeria Touring. Initially, the first bodies were built in Italy by Vignale but this work was later taken back in house to the Midlands.

Externally, the car's most prominent feature was the voluminous curved rear window – it must have measured at least an acre – which formed the tailgate. Remove this door and the space remaining would make an ideal balcony or the basis for a kids' paddling pool.

Celebrity Interceptor owners included John Bonham, Farrah Fawcett and Roger Moore. Most notably, comedian Eric Morecambe owned a 1968 model and had his first heart attack in it that year while driving home after a show – much to the amazement of passer-by Walter Butterworth, who stepped in to drive him, very quickly, to hospital. In 2017, that same car sold at auction for £96,000.

This pristine FF won't be suffring a rear paddling pool conversion anytime soon.

An array of switches and buttons are the centrepiece of the impressive Jensen Interceptor's interior.

Luxurious as well as powerful, these cars had automatic gearing, electric windows, quality stereo and air conditioning as standard. Power steering didn't become a built-in item until 1969, which undoubtedly made light of turning this otherwise heavy motor.

Of the 6,000 made during the model's ten-year life, 320 four-wheel-drive FF models were built, a feature pre-dating the Audi Quattro by several years.

Combined with more stringent American safety laws, the car's thirst – an average of 10–12mpg – would prove the Interceptor's undoing as fuel prices rose in the 1970s. Reliability issues among Mk3 models added to the problems and in 1975 the receivers were called in. They allowed the remaining components to be used to carry production into the following year before finally putting up the shutters. Valiant attempts were made to revive both car and brand in the 1980s but by then it had had its day and sales were few. Some 950 Interceptors remain on and off British roads, according to How Many Left?

RARITY RATING

★★★★★   ALL MODELS

FORD ESCORT MK1

1968–75

I had two second-hand Escort Mk1s in the late 1970s and early '80s. I crashed the first into a camper van and then drove its gold-painted replacement into the ground for a year after, covering 37,000 miles in that time.

To my young mind, they knocked spots off anything British Leyland could offer when it came to reliability and ease of maintenance. My 1.3-litre-powered Escorts held their own on the motorways and took all that was thrown at them – except for that awkward encounter with the parked Bedford Dormobile.

The Escort took over where the Anglia had left off in 1968 and quickly proved a hit, its lightly curving lines a precursor for the more coke-bottle-styled Cortina Mk3 arriving three years later.

No self-respecting souped-up Escort worth its go-faster stripes could hit the tarmac without a set of four Cibie spotlights bolted to the front!

From a mechanical point of view, the Halewood-assembled Escort was a meat-and-two-veg motor. Nothing complicated under the bonnet, good underpinnings and decent space inside. Hidden bits stayed largely rust free.

The well-looked-after interior of an Escort Mk1.

Two-door Escorts are probably more sought after than four-door versions.

The most desirable models were the 1300E, one up from my four-door gold XL, the go-faster RSs and the rally-bred Mexico. The Escort became one of the most successful competitors in this arena, the Mexico being produced to celebrate victory in the 1970 London to Mexico World Cup Rally. A surviving genuine Mexico is among the most sought-after classics today.

Estate models were workhorses and many were bought for fleet use. If your new-fangled colour telly went on the blink, chances were the repair man from Radio Rentals or Granada Visionhire would turn up to your house in one. Countless large and small businesses relied on Escort vans and they were familiar choices for the AA, police forces, gas and electricity boards.

By 1974, Ford was able to announce it had built 2 million Escorts, 60 per cent of which were sold in Britain.

RARITY RATING

★★★ SALOONS, ESTATES AND VANS
★★★★ RS 1600 & 2000
★★★★★ GENUINE MEXICO MODELS

VOLKSWAGEN TYPE 4 (411 & 412)

1968–74

Volkswagen is, of course, best known the world over for the Beetle, but if you wanted a more luxurious product from Wolfsburg, then you could choose the Type 4 saloon and estate (Variant) models.

Retaining a rear-mounted, air-cooled, 1679cc engine, the Type 4 was VW's first four-door saloon – although two-door cars were made as well – and came kitted out with other innovations including unibody construction, coil springs and a hydraulic clutch.

Commercially, the Type 4 should have done better but it was hampered by a lowly 20mpg against a background of rising fuel prices and, later on, a fuel crisis. VW's heart wasn't really in the project anyway; Beetles were still earning the bread and butter in the late 1960s and the company was busy developing the front-engined, water-cooled Passat that would replace the Type 4 during the following decade.

Volkswagen Type 4 four-door saloon.

Inside the Type 4. It's a hard car to spot these days, only seventy being left in the UK.

Type 4s were launched in 1968 with twin carburettors but these were replaced a year later by fuel-injection models that could be readily spotted as they also had twin round headlights, rather than single oval lamps. In the final year of production, carburettors once again took over fuel delivery, this time supplying a 1795cc engine.

The Type 4 was the last VW car design to rely on air cooling – although Beetles continued to be made for many more years in this way – and its demise was assured by the Passat coming on to the market in 1973.

During its six-year run, VW built 367,728 Type 4s and of these around seventy remain on UK roads, according to How Many Left?

Like its Beetle counterpart, the Type 4's engine is in the back.

RARITY RATING

★★★★★ SALOONS AND VARIANTS

AUSTIN MAXI

1968–81

It's easy to condemn the Alec Issigonis-styled Austin Maxi as another of BMC/British Leyland's production disasters but that wouldn't be entirely fair – besides it's more fun to save our opprobrium for the Austin Allegro.

From the mid-1960s onwards, BMC was selling Minis and Austin 1100/1300s as fast as it could make them but had little to offer the family-car market. A rushed and budget-conscious development project took the ungainly Austin 1800 'landcrab', chopped off the rear fins, retained the huge side doors, tarted up the interior and added new badges before painting them mainly in either hearing-aid beige or ginger-biscuit brown. Bright orange and phlegm green were also available from a gaudy colour palette but by then it was the 1970s so nobody minded.

What were firsts, though, for British Leyland by now, were the hatchback opening rear door and a five-speed gear box. This was mated to either a transverse 1500cc (underpowered) or 1750cc engine (not ready until 1970), depending on what you wanted to pay.

The Austin Maxi – this one from 1980 – was British Leyland's larger family car and, despite some early failings in the transmission area, was versatile enough to be a people carrier, double bed or load lugger – as well as offering an air of respectability for its owners of the decade.

A typical view of the Maxi's power plant, although this one has benefitted from a good slathering of underseal around its inner wings.

RARITY RATING

★★★★   ALL MODELS

Oceans of space gave room for five, while the rear seats could be folded for generous load-lugging in a similar way MPVs have done in more recent times. The Ford Cortina estate was one of the few cars that could match the Maxi's carrying capacity.

At the start, Maxis were plagued by problems with the cable-operated gearbox and it took nearly two years for them to be ironed out. By autumn 1970, the Maxi was finally holding its own to become a popular sight on British and European roads – many a family holiday was made, and sometimes broken, by a Maxi packed to the gunwales with children and dogs inside and a mountain of luggage tied to the roof, traversing the growing number of motorways across Britain.

Some half a million Maxis were built until the summer of 1981, with engines and gearboxes being made at Longbridge and shipped to Cowley for final assembly. These days, it's estimated by How Many Left? that there are fewer than 200 remaining on and off Britain's roads – only one is automatic.

RELIANT SCIMITAR GTE

1969–86

It's one of those strange but true facts that the same company that inflicted a plethora of dodgy three-wheelers upon the world also gave us the glamorous, trend-setting Reliant Scimitar GTE.

Some of those three-wheeled frights were even designed by the same guy, Tom Karen of Ogle Design, who styled the Scimitar's lines.

Reliant's success with the Scimitar GTE led the company to widely advertise it as the second-fastest-selling British-made car for a while in the early 1970s – at a time when British Leyland was hampered by endless strikes.

The GTE – standing for Grand Touring Estate – was the first motor to have separate folding rear seats, something so commonplace now you wonder why it took until 1969 to come up with the concept.

Lots of dials and gauges in this tidy Scimitar.

Built with a fibreglass body mounted on to a steel chassis, the Scimitar GTE was powered by a 3-litre V6 Ford engine, giving it a top speed of 120mph. If you opted for overdrive, you could get a creditable 27mpg out of it too.

It found wide appeal among the two-homes set, who thought nothing of chucking a bundle of suitcases in the back before enjoying a weekend retreat from city to country.

The Scimitar found royal favour too. In November 1970 Queen Elizabeth II and the Duke of Edinburgh bought daughter Princess Anne a light blue model as a joint 20th birthday and Christmas present. She would go on to buy several more in the coming years, driving a couple of them rather too quickly for the liking of Mr Plod, who booked her for speeding. The last Scimitar purchased by HRH was also the last built by Reliant in 1986; the company couldn't afford to update this otherwise successful car.

How Many Left? estimates there are still 1,500 GTEs on British roads, while another 2,400 await their turn for rebuilds or refurbishment.

RARITY RATING

★★★★   ALL MODELS

The Scimitar Sabre was the final incarnation of Reliant's grand tourer, this one dating from 1983.

BOND BUG

1970–74

Just over half a century ago, cash-strapped students were the target market for a bright orange, wedge-shaped piece of cheese intended as budget transport.

Slightly cheaper than a Mini (only £9 less, but that was half a week's pay for some in the early 1970s) and at least as much fun to drive, the Bond Bug turned out to be one of the most unorthodox car stylings of the decade.

The obvious difference between it and almost all other cars of the era was that it had only three wheels. It was brought to an unsuspecting public by Bond Cars, of three-wheeler kings, Reliant of Tamworth.

This profile view of the Bug emphasises its wedge outline.

The squared-off rear end of the Bug and its slit-like rear window.

It was penned in the early 1960s by Tom Karen of Ogle Design, who realised there was nothing appealing directly to youngsters devoting their formative years to academia – at least the ones not lost to flower power or smoking pot! – who then bided his time before sharing the idea with Reliant, one of his company's clients.

What later emerged from the factory in 1970 was faithful to Karen's original concept. Built on a Reliant Regal chassis and fitted with a 700cc engine, or 750cc if you had the better-equipped 750ES model, it was poles apart from anything the company had previously made. For a start, it was actually quite quick and could hold its own against the less-powerful versions of Minis and Hillman Imps in a standing start from the neighbourhood traffic lights. Flat out, the Bug could hit 75mph, provided there were no corners involved.

Getting in and out of the Bug was novel too. Undo a catch on the roof and the windscreen, the front and sides opened forward in one piece on hinges set behind the frog-eye-looking headlights. Inside, low seating gave the impression of driving a go-kart.

In all, some 2,200 Bugs were built during the marque's four-year lifespan. How Many Left?

The roof, front windscreen and sides rose as one large piece to enter and exit the two-seat Bond Bug. Note the matching orange steering wheel.

RARITY RATING

★★★★★   ALL MODELS

reckons fewer than 300 survive on the road and in barns today, while all enjoy cult status among devotees. A worthy spot when seen at a local car show – but more likely seen at specialist events.

DATSUN 1200/SUNNY

1970–73

The Datsun 1200/Sunny was one of the storm troopers that helped to turn the British car market upside down in the early 1970s.

Although Datsun, later to become Nissan in the 1980s, had been selling cars in the UK since 1966, it was the second-generation Datsun 1200, better known as the Sunny, alongside the Datsun Cherry, that started whacking some big dents into the sales figures of ailing British Leyland when it made its UK debut in 1970.

The usually loyal British car-buying public learned to swallow its pride over buying foreign cars in the first years of the 'decade that good taste forgot', to the point in 1975 when the government had to plead with Datsun and other Japanese manufacturers to ease off with their imports into the UK.

A four-door example of a 1971-plated Datsun 1200, later to be better known as the Sunny. This second-generation design car would be in the forefront of walloping a strike-prone British motor industry throughout the first half of the decade thanks to its ready availability, keen price and superior standard equipment.

Under the bonnet of a 1971-registered Datsun 1200. Not concours condition but entirely functional – the engine was still good enough to handle a journey from Yorkshire to Kent in 2022 without incident.

Inside the Datsun 1200, still comfy despite signs of wear.

The reason for Datsun's success was simple: while BL and, less frequently, Ford car workers were going on strike, seemingly every other day, their products weren't getting to the showrooms. Waiting lists quickly lengthened. Meanwhile, Sunnys were rolling off the car boats in their thousands, arriving with radios, heated rear windows and clocks as standard equipment and well priced. They were also reliable and economical to run. By 1974, £1,296 bought you a snazzy coupé version.

In common with so many British cars, rust did become an issue, but the ever-resourceful Japanese soon learned how to deal with that. Technologically, the Sunny wasn't particularly advanced, but then it didn't really need to be; 63bhp from the larger 1.4-litre engine was sufficient for most needs.

Not often seen at classic events, the twenty or so Sunnys/1200s that are left are worth seeking out just to appreciate their slightly awkward design looks. The Sunny was Datsun's first global big hitter, shifting 2.3 million worldwide during the first half of the 1970s and paving the way for Japanese domination over the following decades.

RARITY RATING

★★★★★   ALL MODELS

FORD CORTINA MK3

1970–76

Without a doubt, if we had enough space in this book, we could include all five versions of the Ford Cortina, such is the standing of each one in the annals of British classic cars.

As it is, we devote ourselves to the Mk3 model of the rudely named Dagenham Dustbin, which took over from the Mk2 in late 1970. Getting the new motor to the market stalled in early 1971, though, when Ford workers at Dagenham went on strike for eleven weeks, losing an estimated 150,000 cars from production.

A capacious Ford Cortina Mk3 XL estate. Registered near the end of production, it looks smart with its black vinyl roof. Police car versions looked similar to this one.

The Mk3's eventual arrival was a signal marker in design terms for the new decade of Bay City Rollers, impossibly wide-flared trousers, maxi-skirts and Sinclair pocket calculators.

The tow bar and rear fog lamps on the back of this estate suggest it's still working hard more than forty-five years after first taking to the roads.

A wide range of engines, trims and colours helped the Cortina appeal to all budgets, as had the earlier versions. Fleet buyers bought them by the hundred, the importance of their individual users clearly marked out in the corporate pecking order by how many bells and whistles each one came with! If you were a junior sales rep, your 1300cc model would be lucky to have a rev counter. At the top end, the regional manager might get metallic paint, a vinyl roof, flashier wheel trims and a push-button radio cassette player with his, all hauled along by a 1600cc or 2-litre engine.

Spotting this four-door 1972 Mk3 L model was
a real find, such is their scarcity today.

The reliance on the fleet market for a hefty chunk of Cortina sales – around 30 per cent by 1974 – was easily demonstrated by counting how many could be seen of an evening in the car parks of Crest or Trust House Forté hotels alongside Britain's growing number of motorways. Fifteen to twenty lined up in organised rows would not have been unusual.

Load-lugging estate versions were offered for those with a tribe of children to take to school or who were in the habit of demonstrating white goods. Police forces chose Cortinas as area patrol cars too. There were endless permutations to this mile-eater, available in the UK in thirty-five basic versions ranging in price from £914 to £1,338 at launch.

For Ford itself, the Mk3's arrival was a turning point too. It had taken the best part of three years to bring it to market amid much management infighting as British and European arms were merged into one operation. This saw the departure of key members of the UK-based Cortina design team to other carmakers, the drafting in of replacements from Ford USA – leading to the finished car's American-influenced styling – and the rise of the German-built Ford Taunus, essentially the same as the Cortina but with squarer Teutonic flourishes.

Despite a bumpy launch, not helped by quality issues around the poor fitting of doors, the Cortina Mk3 was soon vying for top position as the best-selling car of 1971, narrowly beaten by the Austin/Morris 1100 and the Mini.

Plenty of patina in the engine bay of the Cortina Mk3 means this example is given regular use rather than being forgotten in a garage all year.

The Cortina L interior – note the wide air vents set above the dials.

Remnants of a Ford dealer's rear window sticker.

By 1974 the E Cortina had been revived after Ford bowed to customer pressure, taking over from the range-topping 2000 GXL, actually boasting real wood door cappings and dashboard trim among its enhanced specs. The estate version was particularly well appointed.

October 1975 saw the Mk3 hit its millionth sale when it had already survived longer than its predecessors. It would put on another 100,000 sales before production ended the following year.

The surviving number of Cortina Mk3s can be counted in the low hundreds today, with the GL and GLS models being the most numerous.

RARITY RATING

★★★★   ALL MODELS

HILLMAN AVENGER

1970–81

Launched in Britain in February 1970 as a contender in the fast-growing medium-car market, to take on Ford's Cortina and steal a march on the Morris Marina, the Hillman Avenger was the first Rootes Group car developed under the supervision of Chrysler.

Talks about the car had been kicking around Coventry since the early 1960s but had been overshadowed by problems with the Imp and, later, the resources needed to give birth to the larger Hillman Hunter.

Detroit's design input into the Avenger is clear, with the sloping back lines and J-shaped rear lights being particular stateside influences of the period. Rootes invested a lot of time and money to understand what its customers wanted, many rightly seeing the Avenger as a direct replacement for the familiar Hillman Minx.

The Avenger was first offered with three trim levels, pushed along by either 1250cc or 1500cc engines, and received positive press when it reached the showrooms.

An early 1970s four-door version of the Hillman Avenger GT, perhaps dressed to resemble the Tiger rally sport version, cuts a dash in its orange paint and black vinyl roof combo.

Estate versions of the Avenger were competent load luggers in the 1970s, easily able to hold their own against the Morris Marina.

It proved to be an able alternative to the Morris Marina, in both saloon and estate versions, but was no match for the Mk3 Cortina, which now also boasted a 2-litre option.

A facelift in 1976 was prompted by Chrysler getting jittery amid falling sales, not helped by build-quality issues at Linwood. This was offset by a government-backed rescue plan to keep the company operating in the UK. Vinyl roofs and double lamps on posher models helped prop up sales but a replacement for the Avenger was already in the wings.

From a classic car fan's view, the most exciting Avenger is the Tiger rally sport variant. Initially only sold in bright yellow with a wide black stripe and rear spoiler, the first 100 off the line sold quickly and another 100 followed. A Mk2 Tiger followed in 1972, this time painted in red and given new alloy wheels instead of the previous Minilites. Only 650 Tigers out of a total of 640,000 Avengers were produced. According to How Many Left?, fewer than 300 Avengers, twenty of them Tigers, were still roadworthy in 2022.

From a later example of an Avenger, awaiting a new home, is the more lurid orange and brown interior, colours widely inflicted upon motorists at the end of the 1970s.

RANGE ROVER

1970–96 (FIRST GENERATION)

More than half a century has passed since this leviathan of the road, track and field made its debut in 1970. Aimed squarely at the farming fraternity who wanted something more comfortable than the utility Land Rovers to which they were accustomed, the order books were soon overflowing.

Compared to today's luxury versions, the early bog-busting Range Rover was pretty basic. Rubber floor mats and plastic-covered seats enabled you to sloosh a hose inside the car after a hard day gathering straw and horse poo or giving lifts across mountains to stricken sheep. After that, the Range Rover would come into its own again when taking out one's Significant Other for a slap-up dinner and dance.

The Range Rover created a whole new class of motor (the SUV off-roader) and, with hindsight, British Leyland didn't realise what it had achieved – not for some years anyway, by which time the company was hobbled by huge debts.

Work was started on the Range Rover project in 1966 by a team that included designer David Bache with seasoned engineers Spencer King and Gordon Bashford. Ruggedness was their watchword as they melded permanent four-wheel drive to Rover's powerful 3.5-litre V8 engine, bodywork with aluminium panels and revolutionary styling that won a hatful of awards in its first year. In 1972, the Range Rover was exhibited at the Musée de Louvre in Paris as a shining example of industrial design.

A mid-1970s example of the original two-door Range Rover.

In the days before leather was mandatory in all Range Rovers, crushed velour was used to cover the seats.

Like other BL motors of the era, the parts bin was raided and other components made to suit left- and right-hand-drive versions, the flat dashboard and separate speedo unit being obvious examples.

For eleven years, customers could only order two-door manual models, but a four-door version arrived in 1981, with automatics becoming available for 1983. By then, the Range Rover had some serious competition, most notably from Mercedes, Nissan and Mitsubishi, and while they were bulletproof reliable, they lacked the credentials to appeal to the monied British middle and upper classes.

Range Rover fire engine –
Carmichael converted a number of
Range Rovers into six-wheel fire
engines. (© Brooklands Museum)

Four-wheel-drive sales took off in the 1990s and the Range Rover was in the vanguard of this boom, receiving its first major upgrade in 1994 to become the Classic model. Some models now received air suspension and enough leather upholstery to resemble the reading room of a respectable gentleman's club.

During that twenty-five-year period, an entire after-market had built up in taking basic Range Rovers and adapting them into high-end bespoke gin palaces – commanding eye-watering prices – and giving rise to the 'Chelsea tractor' nickname. The only off-roading they were likely to see was the weekly shopping trip around a supermarket car park or one of the burgeoning out-of-town shopping malls.

Other Range Rovers found a more practical life as police forces throughout the land bought them as patrol or command vehicles. Fire-engine builder Carmichael took the Range Rover as the basis for a six-wheeled appliance for use on smaller airfields, both civil and military. The state visit to Britain by the Pope in 1982 saw him being driven around the country in a custom-built version with a high roof, enabling him to stand up in safety behind strengthened glass.

Production continued at Solihull until early 1996, when no fewer than 317,600 had rolled off its lines. The Range Rover's legacy continues to this day, of course, with the Range Rover Sport, the Range Rover Velar and the Range Rover Evoque being familiar sights.

At classic car shows, look out for off-roading clubs displaying their mud-pluggers and no doubt early Range Rovers will be among them. Thousands survive but some specific editions are nearing extinction today.

RARITY RATING	
★★★★★	OLDER CLASSIC VOGUE V8S
★★★	ALL OTHER MODELS

TRIUMPH STAG

1970–77

Stretch out the 'a' syllable and you have one of the most masculine-named cars ever to have taken to our roads – the Staaaaaag. It's enough to have sane men reaching for long-hidden chest wigs and medallions!

The four-seater convertible Triumph Stag was launched in the summer of 1970, although its design had been knocking around the Italian design studios of Giovanni Michelotti for five years before that.

In a typical British Leyland decision, snatching defeat from the jaws of victory, the company decided its first sports car since formation should be powered by an untried Triumph double-overhead-camshaft, 3-litre V8 engine.

The Stag had few rivals in the market but its nearest was probably the far more expensive Mercedes 350SL. Frustrated early Stag owners might have thought paying the difference would have been worth it though!

The Triumph Stag offered plenty of gauges and dials to keep masculine egos well massaged while at the wheel.

It proved to be the car's Achilles heel, ruining the Stag's reputation for years after. The water pump was high up in the engine and, if the coolant level dropped too low, the engine overheated. Combined with a variety of other quality-control issues, the Stag found itself on a bumpy road among frustrated customers making costly warranty claims.

A well-maintained Stag was generally OK, especially once the engine had been replaced by subsequent owners, often for a Buick-derived Rover V8.

The Stag Mk2, produced from 1973, was far less troublesome. Standard equipment included electric windows, power steering and power-assisted brakes. On later cars the hard top, previously an option, was included in the £2,500 price – as was overdrive.

The car's handsome design has helped it to become a revered classic today, supported by thriving owners' clubs and good parts availability from specialist suppliers.

Just shy of 26,000 Stags were built with 8,100 exported. Today some 8,500 are on or off the road in the UK.

RARITY RATING

★★★ ALL MODELS

MORRIS MARINA & ITAL

1971–84

Looking back over the past decades, the Morris Marina can be fairly viewed as a Marmite car: you either loved it or hated it!

It has been disliked widely enough to have had a piano dropped on one by TV's *Top Gear* team, smashing both car and instrument to pieces, yet is revered enough for the last few hundred remaining examples to lead pampered lives today.

The Marina was designed to be an unpretentious workhorse right from the start, transporting families, salesmen and

Whether rain or shine, the Morris Marina put in solid work for its owners wherever it went.

their belongings around the country without fuss or drama. Not only was there a decent-sized saloon but a perkier coupé and a roomy estate to choose from. The 1800cc twin-carb engine from the MGB and the 1300cc A-series engine powered the various models.

Launched in 1971, it was the first car to be designed by British Leyland with the idea of taking sales from the Ford Cortina, by then just in Mk3 guise, as well as the smaller Ford Escort. To a large extent the Marina succeeded, clocking up a million sales by 1978, second only to the all-conquering Cortina for some time.

Sparing every expense, BL used its parts bins skilfully. Rear axles came from Triumph, while front suspension was adapted from the recently withdrawn Morris Minor. Control knobs, gauges, door and window handles were taken from across the BL range to further pare down costs. All of this kept the price low to customers, who were mainly middle-income families and business people looking for a cheap set of wheels.

By the end of the decade, the Marina's styling was refreshed with help from Italdesign studios and rebadged as the Morris Ital, the last model to bear the Morris name. Van versions of both Marina and Ital sold in quantity to British Telecom and other utility firms, whose contracts kept the commercial vehicle in production for some months after the cars had ceased in 1984.

Morris Marina Coupé, with black vinyl roof. The bonnet is open to show off the engine – not to be confused with being a signal for having broken down!

In addition to the dreaded tin worm, many Marinas and Itals became donor vehicles to more popular BL classics and so, out of 800,000 sold in Britain, only about 1,000 survive on and off road now, the Itals proving especially hard to spot.

Under the bonnet of the more powerful 1.8 Marinas lay a twin-carb engine, also used in MGBs.

The passage of time is proving kinder to the remaining Marinas, now seen as vehicles to be cherished rather than trashed, and there is a wider realisation they weren't so dreadful after all!

RARITY RATING

★★★★ SALOONS AND COUPÉS
★★★★★ ALL ITALS PLUS MARINA VANS, ESTATES AND PICK-UPS

FORD GRANADA MK1

1972-77

The first incarnation of Ford's executive saloon arrived in 1972 from its Dagenham and Cologne factories to replace the ageing Zephyr, quickly establishing itself as the motor of choice for high-achieving regional managers and junior directors.

It gained considerable prominence while used by the good guys on TV's *The Sweeney*, but Ford insisted no crooks or crims should get their thieving mitts on them as it projected the wrong image. Actors John Thaw and Dennis Waterman clearly enjoyed throwing their Granada (actually it was the lesser-appointed Consul) around with aplomb and using the kind of rough language that had clean-up-telly campaigner Mary Whitehouse reaching for her smelling salts.

While there was a range of snazzy colours as well as the obligatory black vinyl roof to choose from, memory suggests that most Granada Mk1s were painted in bronze/ gold or chocolate brown complemented by a tan-coloured plush interior with fake woodwork across the dashboard.

The coupé version of the Ford Granada Mk1, with or without vinyl roof, was an assertive-looking motor. This one had a 2.3-litre engine to back up its looks.

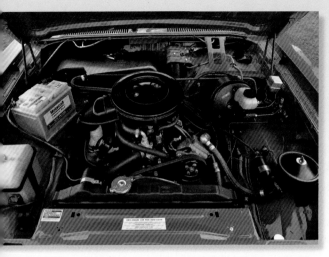

The engine looked as good as the rest of the Granada example spotted in Lincolnshire.

Engine choices were 2-, 2.5-V6 and 3-litre V6. Which one you got probably depended on where you were in the company car fleet pecking order.

These sizeable motors lent themselves particularly well to being chopped in half and a central extension then added to become a spacious limousine, a version that the funeral trade purchased in numbers alongside another Granada conversion into a hearse.

For the rest of us, the Granada was also available as a coupé, marked out by a sharp-sloping rear roof line, as well as a capacious estate. All three Mk1 versions are hard to find, with survivors counted in the low hundreds during 2022.

It may be left-hand drive but it's over here! Cockpit of a 1970s Granada.

RARITY RATING

★★★★   ALL MODELS

RENAULT 5

1972–96

Arriving in the UK from French shores at the tail end of 1972, the Renault 5 offered neat styling and hatchback practicality, making it one of the first superminis.

Volkswagen, Ford, Vauxhall and even British Leyland realised they had some catching up to do when they set eyes upon the R5, but it wouldn't be until at least the middle of the 1970s when they responded with their respective launches of the Golf, Fiesta, Chevette and Metro.

The Renault 5 offered a useful range of engine sizes – 850cc, 950cc, 1100cc, 1289cc and 1397cc – all with a variety of trim levels to opt for at your local dealer. Little wonder the R5 found favour with British buyers tiring of domestic offerings like the Austin 1100 and Hillman Imp.

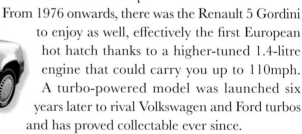

From 1976 onwards, there was the Renault 5 Gordini to enjoy as well, effectively the first European hot hatch thanks to a higher-tuned 1.4-litre engine that could carry you up to 110mph. A turbo-powered model was launched six years later to rival Volkswagen and Ford turbos and has proved collectable ever since.

A four-door version of a later Renault 5, the 1.4-litre Prima edition dating from 1990.

Renault 5s are hard to find today; this one was first registered in Hampshire during 1990.

Looking pristine inside, the Renault 5's wheel and dash followed an angular edge design that was popular at the time.

A Mk2 version of the R5 was launched in early 1985 and, while visually similar, there were a hatful of tweaks and changes to keep the car fresh for another ten years – and ahead of the competition as well. A GT turbo made its debut at the same time, staking Renault's claim for a share of the mid-1980s fast-growing hot-hatch market.

Overall, Renault built and sold 5.5 million 'cinques' worldwide during the model's life, no doubt helped, in the UK of the early 1980s at least, by cheesy TV adverts that sang 'You feel more alive in a 5'. Today, Renault 5s have all but disappeared, with around 750 remaining on our roads, some models being on the point of extinction. Another 3,000 are lingering in barns or garages.

RARITY RATING

★★★★ MOST MODELS
★★★★★ RENAULT 5 GORDINI

AUSTIN ALLEGRO

1973–82

Mention the very name Austin Allegro and you sum up all that was wrong with British Leyland during the first half of the 1970s. The company was effectively moribund, strapped for cash amid plummeting sales and beset by strikes. When the workers did get around to building cars, scant attention was paid to quality control.

It was never meant to be like this. Harris Mann penned this family-sized replacement for the top-selling Austin and Morris 1100/1300 range and made a decent job of it.

Wearing a typical colour of the 1970s era – British Leyland biscuit no less – this Austin Allegro 1100 deluxe has survived well.

Once management had finished tinkering around, though, it was obvious the design had been agreed by committee – and it suffered accordingly. Not for nothing was the Allegro christened the flying pig and, worse, the All Aggro.

British Leyland had a golden opportunity to get ahead of the game but ended up snatching defeat from the jaws of victory yet again – principally by choosing not to make the Allegro a hatchback, just as the market was clamouring for cars with rear-opening doors.

Early Allegros were equipped with the now infamous 'Quartic' square steering wheel to give the driver a better view of the dials. With so much ridicule heaped on the car, it was a feature that was soon dropped.

Undaunted, BL launched the more upmarket Van Den Plas version in 1974. It was defined by a distinctive front grille and an interior featuring leather seats, thick carpets and a walnut dashboard. Not too bad a look so long as you didn't opt for hearing-aid beige or phlegm green – aka Applejack – bodywork.

The estate model arrived in 1975 and turned out to be quite practical – that had a hatchback door, of course.

By the time the Aggro was killed off, some 642,000 had been sold, the majority in the UK but BL managed to inflict some on parts of Europe as well.

For a car so hated at the time – OK, the last ones built in the late 1970s and early '80s weren't nearly as bad – it's remarkable how revered they are today.

On-road survivors total around 270, with fewer than 400 on SORN. Particularly scarce are automatic models and anything with a 1750cc engine, while the Van Den Plas spec is all but extinct, according to How Many Left?

The upmarket version of the Allegro was the Van Den Plas model and its dashboard was given the full walnut treatment. Passengers' *derrières* were cossetted by leather seats.

RARITY RATING

★★★★ BASE AND MANUAL MODELS
★★★★★ 1750CC MODELS, AUTOS AND VAN DEN PLAS MODELS

CHRYSLER ALPINE/ TALBOT SOLARA

1975–85

The all-new Chrysler Alpine was introduced in 1975 to replace the ageing Hillman Hunter. Having been styled in Coventry with running gear developed in Poissy, France, at the former Simca factory, assembly would be carried out at both locations.

The Alpine was an early front-wheel-drive hatchback up against the recently unveiled Volkswagen Passat, Vauxhall Cavalier and Ford's ubiquitous Cortina among others. Clearly it could hold its own as it was named European Car of the Year for 1976.

Spotted in Lincolnshire, this rare Talbot Solara, the booted version of the Alpine, was looking well cared for in 2021.

Three trim levels were available on launch of the Alpine – GL, S and GT – and sales were initially impressive across Europe. France was a notable success, where it was sold as the Simca 1308 and 1309, denoting 1294cc and 1442cc engines. Later in the 1970s, new mid-range models came equipped with electric windows and central locking, both features usually found on more upmarket vehicles.

Chrysler sold its European operations to PSA, owner of Peugeot and Citroën, as the 1970s came to an end, and it wasn't long before that company was taking a closer look at the Alpine range and badging it as the Talbot Alpine.

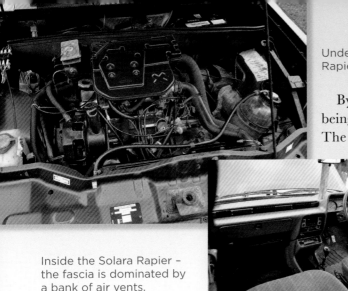

Under the bonnet of a 1985-plated Solara Rapier, the last of the line.

By 1980 a booted version of the car was being produced, known as the Talbot Solara. The Alpine was facelifted at the same time and both cars featured new lights, alloy wheels, headlamp wash/wipe and power steering on the higher-priced versions.

Inside the Solara Rapier – the fascia is dominated by a bank of air vents.

While both cars were stylish and cheaper than their main rivals, quality suffered, particularly some of the push-button switches, which had a habit of dislodging just as you pressed them. Some drivers found the spring-loaded gear change between second and third took a lot of getting used to.

Manufacturing at Ryton ended in 1985 to make way for the Peugeot 309, but the last Solaras and Alpines were given farewell rebadging as the Sunbeam and Rapier to denote higher trim levels.

Nearly as rare as hen's teeth today – the one spotted in Lincolnshire had driven from Scotland the day before – the combined number of Alpines and Solaras on UK roads in 2022 just touches 150, according to How Many Left?

RARITY RATING

★★★★★ ALPINE AND SOLARA, ALL MODELS

TRIUMPH TR7

1975–82

A yellow TR7, first plated in 1981, brightens up a dull day with its pristine wedge-shaped styling.

Introducing the Triumph TR7 was a huge step into a brave new world for British Leyland, allowing it to streamline its ageing sports car line-up and meet the latest legal demands of the long-vital American export market.

In the early 1970s, motor manufacturers were led to believe that open-topped cars would be outlawed stateside on safety grounds by the middle of the decade – and this prompted BL to turn the spotlight on its convertibles bearing MG and Triumph badges and to decide they had had their day.

Internal politics at BL ensured the Triumph brand won out for the new wedge-shaped hard-top coupé, powered by a smooth 2-litre, four-cylinder engine and designed by Harris Mann.

Exports to the US began in 1975 amid positive reviews and, because of high demand there, it would be a full year before the home market saw its first examples.

Left: This convertible's interior looks less lurid than some for having a brown trim teamed with tartan.

Right: A pristine TR8 twin-carb, 2-litre engine.

Those early cars were built at Speke in Liverpool, which, in common with other car plants, saw a good deal of industrial unrest at the time – and that impacted on quality. A common issue was only one of the flip-up headlights rising when switched on – giving a very lopsided look. TR7 production was transferred to Canley near Coventry in 1978 before moving again two years later to Solihull, where the convertible TR8 would emerge in 1979 (the US had vetoed the idea of banning open-top cars after all).

The TR7's design is not everyone's cup of tea, many seeing it as a stereotypical example of dodgy 1970s automotive styling and quality, particularly when viewed in lurid phlegm green. Others see them as avant garde and are quite happy to live with a bright tartan interior wrapped around them. The TR7 has achieved lasting fame in more recent times as a yellow one is the motor of choice for Lance Slater, the character played by Toby Jones in the hugely popular BBC sitcom *Detectorists*.

RARITY RATING

★★★ SALOONS
★★★★ CONVERTIBLES

VAUXHALL CAVALIER

1975–95

By the mid-1970s, the fleet sales market was proving increasingly important to Britain's mainstream carmakers. Vauxhall had been a little late to this party but made up for that by unveiling the Cavalier in November 1975.

The first ones were built at General Motors' factory in Antwerp, Belgium, but demand soon outstripped supply and the decision was taken to add a production line at Vauxhall's plant in Luton. They started rolling off there by March 1977.

The Cavalier name would feature strongly in the British car market until 1995, giving Ford's products a serious run for their money – it was probably the only car capable of snapping at the heels of the Cortina and, later, the Sierra, as it went through upgrades and full facelifts. In fact, Cavalier fleet sales rose sharply after managers saw the Sierra for the first time in 1982. They were put off by its jelly-mould curves and voted with their feet to buy the less racy, yet predictable, Vauxhall instead.

The new front-wheel-drive Mk2 Cavalier arrived in August 1981 and would be the model to pick up sales from the out-of-favour Ford

Boasting a bank of Lucas spot and fog lamps under its front bumper, this late 1970s Mk1 Cavalier is probably ready for anything.

A rarer two-door version of the Mk1 Cavalier dating from 1979.

Vauxhall's Mk1 Cavalier was made with the fleet market in mind and was probably the first car to provide real competition for the Ford Cortina.

offering, helped by having a 1.8-litre engine option in its range that kept it at the bottom end of the newly introduced company-car-tax scale.

A third and final version of the marque landed on these shores in August 1988 with a 4x4 version in the range for the first time. As before, the emphasis was on space, value and trouble-free running. The souped-up model, the SRi, premiered a year or two later to some acclaim among the hot-hatch fraternity.

Like many family and fleet motors, Cavaliers proved a mainstay of the car market and more than a million were registered in Britain throughout the 1980s. And like many of their ilk, whose very familiarity proved their downfall, they are few and far between on the classic circuit today.

How Many Left? reckons there were around 1,400 Cavaliers still on Britain's roads in 2022, with 6,400 more on SORN. Some models are extinct, such as the automatic Cavalier V6 Diplomat and the Cavalier GL Diesel, the last example not having been seen since 2012.

RARITY RATING

★★★★★ ALL MODELS

FORD CAPRI MK3

1978–86

Of the three incarnations of the Ford Capri, the final one was the most familiar. It lasted eight years in the UK – the same length of time as the two earlier versions added together.

Originally intended by Ford to be the European Mustang, the Capri had a keen following in Britain and the Mk3 was quick to maintain that lead.

Unveiled in 1978, the Capri Mk3 now had quad headlights set in an aeroflow grille – a feature found elsewhere in the Ford range – and a bonnet drawn out over the top of the lamps to give a more dominant

Judging by the 1986 number plate, this Ford Capri Mk3 2.8-litre injection model would have been among the last to be made.

expression. Engines and trim levels from the previous model were carried across. Parts sharing from the Cortina and Escort ranges had helped keep down costs, styling changes bringing a family resemblance to them all.

The dashboard layout of this mid-1980s example was little different from those made ten years earlier.

In spite of its Jack-the-lad/Jackie-the-lass looks, the Capri was actually quite a practical car. Its hatchback opened on to foldable rear seats that would accommodate medium-sized children, dogs and bags of shopping. Most sales were to private owners but in 1982 I swung one as a company car, simply because the smarter 1.6GL was a tenner less than my benchmark Cortina 1.6L! Although reliable, the interior was looking a little dated by then – even so, young ladies of my acquaintance were still impressed.

Arrival of the 2.8 injection in 1982 extended the Capri's life and by 1984 RHD Lasers for the British market were the only ones still being made. Last off the German production line in December 1986 was the 280 Brooklands model, of which 1,089 were built. Tickford also sold a heavily modified batch of eighty as a final tribute to the Capri – seven of these are thought to survive.

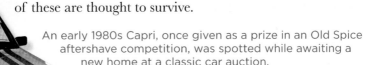

An early 1980s Capri, once given as a prize in an Old Spice aftershave competition, was spotted while awaiting a new home at a classic car auction.

RARITY RATING

★★★ ALL STANDARD MODELS
★★★★ 2.8L AND 280 BROOKLANDS
★★★★★ CAPRI TICKFORD

AUSTIN MINI METRO/MG METRO/ROVER METRO/ ROVER 100

1980–98

Billed as a British car to beat the world, the Austin Mini Metro was also the car desperately needed to bring back some credibility to strike-hit, cash-strapped British Leyland. Amazingly, it did the trick, with 1 million plus sales proving a consistent earner as car and company changed names and owners during an eighteen-year production run.

The hatchback Metro was meant to replace the Mini but the latter's sales held up well enough to rule that out. Perhaps against better advice, the Metro shared the Mini's A-series engine and gearbox, but the new model did bring some useful features to the party, giving arch-rivals the Ford Fiesta and Renault 5 a run for their money.

There was plenty of interior space – enough for a six-footer to enjoy without scraping the headlining anyway – and it had good road manners. The rear seat could

A well-cared-for mid-1980s four-door Austin Metro 1.3L.

Inside an uber rare Rover Metro convertible.

be folded down 60:40, still a relatively new idea in 1980. Two engine sizes were available, the 1 litre and 1.3 litre.

By 1982, the Metro got the turbo treatment with the unveiling of an MG version. This came complete with red seat belts, red carpets and alloy wheels. A genuinely quick small car, it has become sought after in recent years and examples have climbed in value.

The Metro stole a march over rivals in the mid-1980s when a five-door model rolled out of the Longbridge factory for the first time. The rear passenger doors had been cleverly shaped, enabling the body to remain in the same wheelbase.

More than a million Metros, rechristened the Rover 100 from 1990, would be sold by the end of the century and the model regularly held a top-five place in the UK sales charts.

Good runners are hard to find, with the MG and classy Van Den Plas versions being the classic owners' favourites.

According to How Many Left?, in 2022 there were around 2,500 of all versions in road-going order and, surprisingly, another 6,800 languishing in dark corners.

Red stripes on the seats and door cards – as well as the octagon logo on the steering wheel – denote the interior of the much-sought-after MG Metro.

RARITY RATING

★★★★ AUSTIN METRO AND ROVER 100 MODELS
★★★★★ MG METRO TURBO AND VAN DEN PLAS MODELS

DELOREAN DMC12

1981–82

Forever immortalised in the *Back to the Future* movies, the DeLorean DMC12 was the brainchild of renegade General Motors executive John Z. DeLorean.

In 1977 he announced he would build a new luxury sports car. By 1980 you could choose to have yours plated in 24-carat gold, raising the standard price from $25,000 to $85,000 – incredibly, seven orders were placed but never made.

Production of stainless-steel-finished DMCs finally began in January 1981 at a purpose-built factory in Dunmurry, Belfast. The British government gave around £60 million in grants, anxious to create jobs in the troubled province.

The DMC won mixed reviews. The distinctive gull-wing doors were nothing short of a sensation but a 0–60mph time of 10.5 seconds appeared a tad slow for a car in this price category. Sales didn't match expectations and matters were further hampered by quality issues. An extensive support network was set up in the US to ensure factory-fresh cars were in good enough order before release to the dealers, let alone the customers.

A wide black side stripe gives this DeLorean a muscular stance.

The DeLorean's power plant.

Production faltered and came to an end amid financial difficulties in December 1982. By then some 9,000 DMCs had been built.

Today, around 6,000 are thought to survive, mostly in the US, where owners can rely on a good replacement parts network, largely thanks to the surplus components being bought up when the company closed. A handful of DMCs reside in the UK and do make an occasional appearance at car shows – there is at least one kitted out with *Back to the Future* time-travel accessories. As yet, though, the flux capacitor is non-operational!

Finally spotted one! Inside a *Back to the Future* example of the DeLorean that appeared at a show in Ramsgate, Kent, during 2022.

RARITY RATING

★★★★ FACTORY STANDARD
★★★★★ *BACK TO THE FUTURE*

TRIUMPH ACCLAIM

1981–84

A 1984 Triumph Acclaim in well-cared-for condition – with the benefit of a pair of front fog lamps.

It would be easy to dismiss the Triumph Acclaim merely as a Japanese wolf in British sheep's clothing, but to venture partners Honda and British Leyland it proved a mutually worthwhile milestone.

By the beginning of the 1980s, BL was drinking in the last-chance saloon, desperately hoping the Metro would turn its fortunes around. Now it needed a medium-sized motor to replace the outdated models still cluttering up its dealers' showrooms. Officially, the Acclaim would replace the Dolomite, but the Allegro, Ital and Maxi were also ripe for the chop.

The Acclaim wasn't particularly revolutionary but the deal between BL and Honda, known as Project Bounty, certainly was. It was the first time British and Japanese rivals had worked together and centred around building the four-door Honda Ballade under licence at Cowley near Oxford. The 1300cc twin-carb engines and five-speed gearboxes were imported from Japan, while the remaining components were sourced and made in the UK –

Under the Acclaim's bonnet.

this was at least 70 per cent by value, which allowed the Acclaim to be considered a fully fledged British car.

They turned out to be decently equipped, well-screwed-together motors, if not a little cramped for Western-world families. They found favour among older drivers who weren't bothered by lack of speed but more interested in reliability and frugality – 32mpg was usual.

At last, BL could hope for better times, while Honda, already finding success with the Civic and Accord, gained a firmer foothold in Britain. The Acclaim's life may have been comparatively short at three years, but it did notch up some 133,000 sales and holds the record for the lowest number of BL warranty claims.

They are rare beings today and you may be hard put to see one on display – barely more than 100 were roadworthy in 2022, with another 270 lurking in garages and barns, according to How Many Left?

Crushed velour seats, electric windows and a cubby hole for loose change are among the features inside the posh model of the Triumph Acclaim.

RARITY RATING

★★★★★ ALL MODELS

FORD SIERRA

1982-93

'Jelly mould' was how this car was quickly described. Its unveiling at the British International Motor Show in September 1982 revealed the Ford Sierra was designed for the fleet market. Initially, it proved too much of a revelation for bewildered bulk buyers, who promptly bought Vauxhall Cavaliers instead.

A mid-1980s GL model of the Ford Sierra in all its jelly-mould styling glory.

The cockpit of a top-of-the-range Sierra Ghia automatic, first registered in 1990.

The hatchback Ford Sierra, the blue oval's replacement for the much-loved Cortina, was off to a rocky start, but with a light facelift a year or so after launch, the fleet buyers were gradually wooed back.

It's true that, while its curvy external styling was like nothing else, the Sierra's drivetrain and underpinnings, transferred from the Cortina,

Hard to find these days is the estate version of the Sierra – this one was spotted at a Kent classic car auction, where it hopefully found a new home and possible restoration.

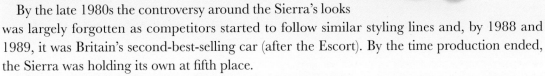

were deliberately conservative in the belief that the fleet market wanted reliability above all else. Offered with a range of engines and increasing numbers of fitted extras, depending on your place in the corporate pecking order, an estate version was unveiled, followed by the booted Sierra Sapphire.

By the late 1980s the controversy around the Sierra's looks was largely forgotten as competitors started to follow similar styling lines and, by 1988 and 1989, it was Britain's second-best-selling car (after the Escort). By the time production ended, the Sierra was holding its own at fifth place.

Sports variations entered the range as well before the 1980s were out – initially the XR4i and the all-wheel-drive XR4x4, which borrowed Ford's V6 from the Granada to hurtle it along. A rally-bred Sapphire version adapted by Cosworth topped the tree and has become a precious entity in the past few years, attracting prices at auction that rival those of middle-market Jaguar E-types.

Some 1.3 million Sierras were made at Ford's plants in Dagenham, Belgium and Germany for the British market alone but very few are on the road now. Usually it's the hot-hatch models gaining the most attention, with the more everyday models harder to spot; if they had survived much into the twenty-first century, they often weren't worth restoring. How Many Left? suggests there are fewer than 2,500 all told on Britain's roads today but, perhaps incredibly, there are another 11,000 lurking in dark corners of barns and garages.

RARITY RATING

★★★★ XR4, XR4X4, COSWORTH MODELS
★★★★★ STANDARD HATCHBACKS, ESTATES AND SALOONS

INDEX OF CARS

Austin/Morris 1100 & 1300   62
Austin A30 & A35   18
Austin Allegro   110
Austin Cambridge   52
Austin Healey 100 & 300   24
Austin Maxi   84
Austin Mini/Morris
    Mini-Minor/The Mini   48
Austin Mini Metro/MG Metro/
    Rover Metro/Rover 100   120
Austin Nash Metropolitan   34

Bond Bug   88
Borgward Isabella   28

Chrysler Alpine/
    Talbot Solara   112
Citroën 2CV   6
Citroën DS   30
Citroën Light 15/
    Traction Avant   8

Daimler Conquest   26
Daimler Dart SP250   42
Datsun Sunny 1200/Sunny   90
DeLorean DMC12   122

Fiat 500   36
Ford Anglia   44
Ford Capri Mk3   118
Ford Cortina Mk3   92
Ford Escort Mk1   80
Ford Granada Mk1   106
Ford Sierra   126

Hillman Avenger   96
Hillman Imp   70
Hillman Minx   32

Jaguar E-Type   56
Jaguar Mk2   46
Jensen Interceptor   78

Land Rover   10
Lotus Europa S1 & S2   72

MGB Roadster & GT   66
Morris 1100 & 1300   62
Morris Marina & Ital   104
Morris Mini-Minor/the Mini   48
Morris Minor   14
Morris Oxford &
    Austin Cambridge   52

Peerless GT 2 Litre   38

Range Rover   98
Reliant Scimitar GTE   86
Renault 4   58
Renault 5   108
Rover 2000 P6   74
Rover P5   40

Triumph Acclaim   124
Triumph Herald   54
Triumph Spitfire & GT6   68
Triumph Stag   102
Triumph TR7   114

Vauxhall Cavalier   116
Vauxhall Viva HA   76
Volkswagen Beetle   20
Volkswagen Type 4
    (411 & 412)   82
Volvo P1800   60